Brecht and The Bible

UNIVERSITY OF NORTH CAROLINA
STUDIES IN THE GERMANIC LANGUAGES
AND LITERATURES

Initiated by RICHARD JENTE (1949–1952), established by F. E. COENEN (1952–1968)

SIEGFRIED MEWS, Editor

Publication Committee: Department of Germanic Languages

For other volumes in the "Studies" see pages 106–07.

Send orders to: (U.S. and Canada)
The University of North Carolina Press, P. O. Box 2288
Chapel Hill, N.C. 27514
(All other countries) Feffer and Simons, Inc., 31 Union Square, New York, N.Y. 10003

NUMBER NINETY-SIX

UNIVERSITY
OF NORTH CAROLINA
STUDIES IN
THE GERMANIC LANGUAGES
AND LITERATURES

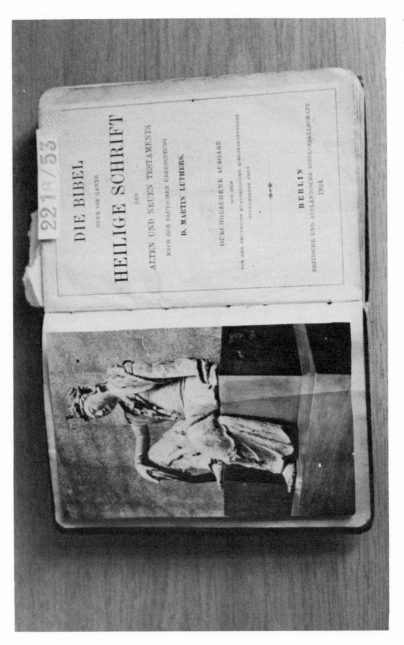

The "frontispiece" discovered in Brecht's pocket Bible glued in opposite the title page. The general attitude of the relaxed buddha seems well chosen and placed for permanent confrontation with *Die Heilige Schrift*. (photo by the author)

Brecht and The Bible

A Study of
Religious Nihilism and Human Weakness
in Brecht's Drama
of Mortality and the City

by
G. RONALD MURPHY, S.J. 1938-

THE UNIVERSITY OF NORTH CAROLINA PRESS
CHAPEL HILL
1980

Library of Congress Cataloging in Publication Data

Murphy, G   Ronald, 1938–
      Brecht and the Bible.

(University of North Carolina studies in the Germanic
languages and literatures; no. 96 ISSN 0081-8593)
Includes bibliographical references.
1. Brecht, Bertolt, 1898–1956—Religion and ethics.
1. Title. II. Series: Studies in the Germanic
languages and literatures (Chapel Hill, N.C.); no. 96.
PT2603.R397Z7856   832'.912   80-20207
ISBN 0-8078-8096-5

Matri Patrique

*

Parentibus Academicis

Fr. Hill   Mrs. Moon   Prof. Hatfield
Prof. Grimm

*

Dilectissimis

*

Amicoque Augustae Vindelicorum
Scribae

Contents

Acknowledgments

All authors are deeply indebted people. I would like to acknowledge my indebtedness to those whose kindness, patience, and encouragement helped make it possible to write this book: my family, Jim McKee, Gene d'Aquili, Jim Devereux, Roger Bensky, Kurt Jankowsky, Reinhold Grimm, Ralph Ley, Joyce Bouvier, Herta Ramthun, and many others, including my indefatigable editor Siegfried Mews, and Richard Lawson.

I would like to thank Suhrkamp Verlag, Frankfurt am Main, for their permission to quote from Brecht's *Gesammelte Werke in 20 Bänden*, copyright © 1967. The *Brecht-Archiv* in East Berlin was most helpful in many ways, especially in giving me permission to take photographs of relevant parts of the copy of Brecht's Bible in their possession.

Finally, I wish to express my gratitude to Stephan Brecht for his permission to publish one of those photographs. The confrontational frontispiece which Brecht glued into his Bible directly opposite the title page, is thus able to be the frontispiece for this book on Brecht's lifelong confrontation with the Bible.

G. Ronald Murphy, S.J.
Glenn Dale, Maryland
May, 1980

Brecht and The Bible

I

Introduction: The Problem

"Sie werden lachen: die Bibel."[1] This mysterious but well-known Brechtian utterance, so often taken as another example of his irony with its emphasis on *lachen*, is a statement that, more than any other, grants jocularly veiled access to the deepest and longest lasting literary influence in Brecht's lifetime of writing. Despite this clue as to what may well be the most significant level of Brecht's thought, few critics have undertaken any systematic exploration of his use (and abuse) of the Bible.[2] Most authors are content to acknowledge biblical influence in the realm of Brecht's language,[3] and only a few seriously point the way to what may be lying beyond phonology.

The language of Brecht's drama is, I believe, the most important in the twentieth century, but the continual conflict in basic understanding and in critical interpretation of his works reveals that there is something enigmatic about the style, and content, of Brecht's works that results in controversy even among well-intentioned contemporary critics and perhaps causes his contemporaries to miss the level on which he is frequently speaking.

Bertolt Brecht was raised in a mixed Catholic-Protestant household. His father, Berthold Friedrich, was a Catholic from the Black Forest, and his mother, Sophie Brezing, was a Protestant. Eugen Berthold was confirmed in the biblical Lutheran tradition of his mother, something which may indicate either deep religious differences within the house, or weakness or generosity on the part of the father.[4] There is little information on this question, but one is more than justified in speculating that the presence of religious dualism in the Brecht family, far more than Hebbel's *Judith*,[5] gave Brecht the first incentive to write *Die Bibel* with its Catholic-Protestant conflict, in which the willingness of the "weak" father to compromise principle for the sake of peace and life is defended, and the hard righteousness of the Bible-reading grandfather is opposed.[6] Another author, writing on the problem of Brecht's antagonism to the middle class, has also come to the conclusion that the Brecht household was extremely important, though in relation to a different question:

Erinnerungen an das Elternhaus finden sich nirgendwo. Man kann es able-
sen nur an den Protestreaktionen des jungen Brecht. Betrachtet man Photos
von Brechts Vater, eines biederen und tüchtigen Direktors einer Papierfabrik,
oder Bilder des kleinen Berthold Eugen, eines pfiffigen Bürschchens mit run-
den lebendigen Augen, in sauberem Matrosenkragen, so kann man sich des
Gedankens nicht erwehren, daß Brechts fanatischer Haß auf die Bourgeoisie
in diesem Elternhaus seine bestimmte Ursache haben müsse.[7]

One might not be going too far in speculating that the mere existence of a perhaps subtle Catholic-Protestant dialectic at home between the father's and the mother's families may not only have given
the inspiration and the point of view for the religious conflict of *Die
Bibel* and of *Mutter Courage*, but also may have first conditioned the
mind of the young Brecht to dialectic and relativistic thinking in general—and given it the oscillating restlessness that would always seek
truth but never seem to be content with any single-minded, absolute
system of truths.

The Bible itself, written as a collection of religious truths, but un-
wittingly the object of "religious" conflict, was Brecht's earliest source
for dramatic material. This is true not only for *Die Bibel*, but for other
early plays as well, most of which we do not now have. Brecht read the
Bible continually as a constant source from which to draw dialectic
conflict:

In seinen Erinnerungen an Brechts Augsburger Zeit im Jahre 1919 hat H. O.
Münsterer [in *Panorama*, Munich, August 1959, pp. 7–8] von zwei nahezu
fertigen Dramen aus jener Zeit berichtet: "Das eine dieser Dramen führt
anfangs den Titel *David oder der Beauftragte Gottes*, der später in *Absalom und
Bathseba* abgewandelt wurde." Der Stoff ist aus der Bibel entnommen, die
Brecht bekanntlich immer wieder las und deren Stil von ihm in manchen
Arbeiten nachgebildet wird. David ist bei aller aus der Heiligen Schrift er-
sichtlichen Immoralität der Mann Gottes. Die Eingangsszene zeigt Absalom
im Burghof, den Soldaten der Leibwache zuhörend, die sich über die Schliche
des alternden Königs recht anrüchige Histörchen erzählen. Da erscheint oben
auf der Mauer David, eine riesige Silhouette. "Ich will Abrechnung halten
mit meinem Sohne Absalom!" Beklemmende Stille, Vorhang, eine Exposition
also, wie sie Brecht in seinen Meisterjahren nicht wirkungsvoller hätte geben
können.[8]

Biblical material can be seen not only in the early plays, but thinly
disguised throughout the later plays as well, for example, the Abraham and Lot story (Genesis 18:20–19:29) in *Der gute Mensch von Sezuan*, and in Solomon's decision (1 Kings 3:13–28) in *Der kaukasische
Kreidekreis*.

In using the Bible in this way, Brecht is far from doing something
out of the ordinary, but rather conforming to a common and one of

the oldest tendencies of German men of letters. For instance, Brecht's more conservative contemporaries, Thomas Mann (the *Joseph* novels) and Hermann Hesse (*Siddhartha, Demian*) also made extensive hermeneutic use of the Bible, although both possess a cooler, more distanced literary relationship to it than does Brecht. Nietzsche's superman competes with the Scriptures in an agonistic trial of superiority. Goethe's *Faust* is, in many respects, from the angelic choirs and the Dies Irae, from the "Christ ist erstanden" to the "Her zu mir," unthinkable without the biblical tradition. Schiller's Karl and Franz Moor play out their roles in a version of the Prodigal Son that rivals the original in intensity if not in brevity. Lessing's Three-Rings theme is a protest against religious wars and intolerance and is remarkably akin in general thrust to *Die Bibel* and *Mutter Courage*. Less veiled is the religious tradition in the Baroque and in Reformation literature where Luther's Bible became the work that formed modern literary German. But when one goes back to *Parzifal* and medieval German, one finds oneself in a much older, almost patristic, tradition of the use of the Bible. Here the hero is not so much the focus of moral struggle or the victim of social circumstance, but, as in *Oedipus*, he is guilty of not realizing who and where he is, of not realizing that he is at the very table of God when he is there. Brecht, it seems to me, in his use of the Crucifixion and Death, is thematically quite close to this older point of view of Sophocles and Wolfram.

In any case, there is a long German literary tradition, only briefly sketched here, of writers using the Bible, overtly and covertly, in such a way that the sacred and the profane are closely mixed. The proportions and the purpose of the mixture are always different, according to the style and intent of the author. Brecht's particular way of using the Bible is the fundamental question this book seeks to answer.

When King Edward is about to be betrayed to his enemies in *Leben Eduards des Zweiten von England* because of his homosexual affair with Gaveston, the audience is suddenly met with a strange sequence of events. The betrayer, Baldock, is trying to think of how to hand the king over to his pursuers. He says to Mortimer, the king's enemy: "Die Bibel lehrt uns, wie's zu halten ist. / Wenn Eure Leute kommen mit Handfesseln und / mit Riemen, will ich zu ihm sagen: Lieber Herr / beruhigt Euch, da habt Ihr ein Handtuch. Und dem / ich dann das Handtuch reiche, der ist es."[9]

When Baldock comes to the king's hiding place, he is invited to share the king's supper: "Trink unser Wasser mit uns, iß unser / Salz und Brot" (GW, I, 251). The tired King Edward declares that "alles ist eitel" (GW, I, 252), and then lays his head on the Abbot's lap. A noise is suddenly heard and, though Spencer says it is just the wind and snow, Baldock says, "Ich daehte, es sei ein Hahnenschrei" (GW, I, 253). Spencer alludes then to sleepiness as promising no good, when suddenly soldiers appear and ask the question: "Wer unter euch ist der König?" (GW, I, 254).

After Spencer's denial that there is a king present, the drama reads: "Baldock *geht auf Eduard zu*: Nehmt dieses Tuch, ich bitt Euch, lieber Herr. / Ihr habt Schweiß auf Eurer Stirn" (GW, I, 254). The king is then seized but: "*Eduard im Abgehen, zwischen Bewaffneten, sieht Baldock an. Baldock weint*" (GW, I, 254).

The entire situation of the Last Supper, the Agony in the Garden and the Arrest has been reset, and brings about a deliberate confusion of the audience's feelings toward the king, whom the audience has been allowed to keep in less-than-polite disrespect up until this point. Why does Brecht use the Bible in this way? Is he satirizing the Bible or even more deeply mocking Eduard's delusions? Why does the audience react subconsciously to the transformed version of the Passion with sympathy and not with rejection?

Brecht scholars do not enter into this discussion frequently, perhaps put off too quickly from a study of his use of the Bible because of their prior knowledge of the author as "the atheist and blasphemer Brecht." As perceptive a theological literary critic as Paul Konrad Kurz, S. J. can only write in a general way of *Mutter Courage*: "Eine der Vergänglichkeit zugeordnete Tiefenschicht Brechts—aus der schon Baal und eine große Anzahl der frühen Gedichte lebten—wird sichtbar, Elementares, das sich wehrt im Streit mit der Umwelt, im Streit mit dem Sterben, . . . eine innerweltlich unwiderlegbar anti-Salomonische Desillusionierung."[10] He even notes in his section on Brecht as *Der Unbequeme*: "Von frühen Jahren an begleitete Brecht das Bewußtsein des Sterbenmüssens. Seine Baal-und-Villon-Lyrik enthält als stets anwesende Partner zwei unheimliche Gestalten: Gott und Tod."[11] Despite this rather accurate analysis, Kurz fails to specify the literary patterns or images in which God is always present as a partner of death.

Reinhold Grimm must be given the credit for first giving proper emphasis to the role of the Bible in Brecht's works and assembling long lists of examples to prove his point. In the chapter in which he discusses Brecht's theory and practice of citation he writes:

Die meisten Belege freilich stammen aus der Bibel: "Nun, mein Sohn, herein mit dir zu deinem Feldhauptmann and setz dich zu meiner Rechten." "Ich kenne den Elephanten nicht." "An den Wassern des Michigansees/Sitzen wir und weinen" . . . Schließlich neigt das parodistische Element dazu, sich zu verabsolutieren: "Als die Herren ächzend und mit Mienen, als unterschrieben sie das Todesurteil für ihre liebsten Anverwandten, ihre Namen auf das

Papier gesetzt hatten, gingen sie schnell auseinander, ein jeglicher in seine Stadt."[12]

Grimm's theory is that Brecht's use of the Bible is a device of *Verfremdung*, an attempt to revive a cliché by the shock of seeing it either "slightly" altered or in an entirely different situation from its original context. This is done, he believes, most frequently in parody of the original meaning (as is certainly true in the examples he cites above). He also notes a more serious Brechtian use of the Bible:

Man darf hier nichts verharmlosen. Wenn die Soldaten im pestverseuchten Florenz die Gasse, wo Galilei wohnt, absperren—eine notwendige, aber für die Betroffenen unmenschliche Maßnahme—bemerkt der Forscher bitter: "Sie hauen uns ab wie den kranken Ast eines Feigenbaumes, der keine Frucht mehr bringen kann." Unter solchen Umständen zitiert, richtet sich das Bibelwort gegen sich selber.[13]

Although Grimm does not like the seriousness of such an attack on the New Testament, he does seem to indicate that it is almost an attack from *inside* the Bible, a kind of internal conflict within the Bible suddenly exposed. Brecht stings the reader by exposing the occasional incidents of apparent or real indifference or cruelty in the Book that is read, in his view, far too mindlessly by its cultural and religious followers. Thus in addition to the type of use to which biblical allusion is put in the Eduard-Baldock scene, where it is used to elicit sympathy for the king's situation, we see Brecht also has a second style of usage. Brecht occasionally sets up serious conflicts between different parts of the Bible, including parts of the New Testament against parts of the Old Testament. This second use of the Bible, then, puts the Bible into a dialectic relationship with itself; but is this poetic delight in blasphemous dialectic, or an attempt to "wake up the class"?

In referring to the incident in the *Dreigroschenoper* where Macheath looks at Brown, and Brown "weeps bitterly" (GW, I, 446), Grimm gives his theory as to Brecht's underlying purpose in so using the Bible—blasphemy:

Das biblische Muster verfremdet den Vorgang im Stück; zugleich aber bedeutet die Wahl dieses Musters eine extreme und durchaus mit beabsichtigte Blasphemie: die Spannungen zwischen den beiden Bereichen wirken dialektisch. . . . So sehr Brecht als Dichter aus der Sprache der (Luther-) Bibel gelernt hat, seine Haltung zu ihrer Botschaft ist kompromißlos ablehnend.[14]

Here, I believe, Grimm may have been misled both by the randomness of the examples he selected from Brecht and by a too univocal concept of the Bible as "a" book, having one single undifferentiated message.[15] Although Brecht does indeed use parts of the Bible many

times in the parodistic and blasphemous—and often humorous—
way Grimm demonstrated, there are other parts of the Bible whose
message Brecht uncompromisingly accepts. It is my conviction that
his negative attitude to the messages of Genesis and the Resurrection
accounts, for example, is not at all the same as his attitude to other
books of the Old Testament such as Ecclesiastes, or to the Crucifixion
accounts of the New Testament whose message he is only too ready
to accept, and to use. The fact that Brecht is able to accept certain
parts of the Bible based on their specific content has also been noted
by Barbara Woods. Commenting on such passages as Brecht's use of
"you shall not bind the mouth of the ox that is threshing the grain,"
she says: "For the tendency of the critics is to concede that Brecht is
indebted to Biblical style, but to assume that his avowed atheism
leads him to reject all Biblical teachings. . . . After all, the Bible contains a good deal of material not strictly theological, such as practical
and moral precepts; and Brecht finds little cause to dispute such
Biblical sayings."[16] This, at least, is the burden of my own conten-
tions concerning Brecht's use of the Bible, though I would go beyond
the practical and moral precepts of the Bible.

Thomas O. Brandt holds a similar opinion to that of the earlier
Grimm, except that he holds the purpose of Brecht's use to be provo-
cation rather than blasphemy, and protest against rather than denial
of too-easily-held faith: "Den bequemen, traditionellen, unerwor-
benen Glauben zu zerstören, daran lag ihm."[17]

The only full-length studies of this entire question, however, are a
dissertation by Gary Neil Garner[18] and Hans Pabst's *Brecht und die
Religion*.[19] Unfortunately, though, Garner does not undertake the
exhaustive internal analysis of the plays that the resolution of this
question demands, but instead begins and ends with an a priori
philosophical approach that tends to deduce Brecht the poet from
nineteenth-century German philosophy. Pabst's book is a much more
thorough and satisfactory work though it also suffers from seeing
Brecht from a too sociologically restricted perspective. Not too surprisingly, Garner and Pabst come to the conventional conclusion that
Brecht is a kind of unoriginal nineteenth-century Marxist-humanist
using drama and the Bible as a means of propaganda. That there is
some truth in such a view, no one will deny, but it does little to
explain such figures as Kattrin, Baal, Paul Ackermann, and Grusche.
The poetic problem itself of the nagging persistence of certain specific
parts of the Bible in many of Brecht's plays remains.

The poetic and stylistic problem of the almost fixed recurrence of
certain phrases and events of biblical "drama" and their almost constant association with the protagonist(s) and his fate, results in the

often-observed, but supposedly prohibited, audience sympathy with Brecht's heroes and heroines. Henry Hatfield has expressed this paradox quite clearly:

A whole battery of devices aims at "distancing" the spectator. Characters step out of their roles, wear masks, or comment on the action. . . . Slogans are projected onto a screen or written placards; some witty, some, in the didactic works, almost insultingly simplistic, which again serves to alienate the audience. . . .

Precisely the best of Brecht's dramas, however, often conflict with these theories. The fortitude of Mother Courage, the goodness of the Chinese prostitute Shen Te, and above all the devotion of Grusche (in *Kreidekreis*) evoke our sympathy, quite in a traditional sense.[20]

This traditional sympathy can not be explained in terms of pure *Verfremdungstheorie*. Can the biblical context of each of these dramatic actions be a covert means of transcending the estrangement without destroying it?

Hans Mayer, remarkably enough in view of his sometime Marxist background, is the person most responsible for advancing the question of the importance of the Bible for Brecht beyond the status first given to it by Reinhold Grimm. Referrring again to the use of Peter's denial of Christ, he comments: "Natürlich steht in alledem viel mehr als eine bloße, durch Zitat fixierte Anspielung. Mit Recht sieht Reinhold Grimm in den meisten Bibelzitaten eine Anwendung des Verfremdungsprinzips, ein dialektisches Reizverhältnis zwischen Ursprung und Aktualisierung des Bibelworts."[21] He is led to go further by the text of a cantata written by Brecht in 1949 for the composer Gottfried von Einem, in an attempt to determine Brecht's standpoint. Mayer cites the cantata text below and then comments:

> "Schaut's, jetzt hat er ihn durchstochen!
> Schaut's, der starke Folterknecht!
> Schaut's, er hat die Wahrheit g'sprochen!
> G'schieht ihm recht! G'schieht ihm recht!"

Das ist nicht der Standpunkt des Evangelisten, wie in der Matthäus-Passion, es ist auch kein mitteilender Kommentar. Die Passion wird von außen gesehen, von der Menge her, die in schauriger Bewunderung für den Folterknecht, auch ein bißchen verächtliches Mitleid für das Opfer aufbringt.[22]

Mayer has perceived the location of the point of view of the writer of the cantata as being within the Gospel scene, but shockingly (and estrangedly) enough, among the distracted crowd who, too easily fascinated by the powerfulness of the guard, do not realize what is happening. He then modifies his agreement with Reinhold Grimm's earlier thesis on Brecht's use of the Bible: "Blasphemie, Anspielung, Verfremdung. Trotzdem ist da noch mehr."[23]

It is my purpose to get at this "noch mehr." This is a somewhat delicate task, since Brecht's usages of the Bible may be "Rufe aus der Tiefe, aber nicht empor zu irgendeinem 'O Herr.' "[24]

This, of course, brings us to the serious problem of Brecht's atheism, and the question of how an atheist could possibly make sincere use of any part of the Bible. Brecht's atheism, in his earlier years at least, is partially a denial, as he put it, of the God of romanticism and of war: "Gott, das war das hohe C der Romantik. Der Abendhimmel über dem Schlachtfeld, die Gemeinsamkeit der Leichen, ferne Militärmärsche, der Alkohol der Geschichte . . . die Zuflucht der Sterbenden und der Mörder" (GW, XX, 4).

Brecht's primeval, pre-Marxist concern about the God of those who die, not just because of an enemy's stroke, but because of an enemy even more primitive and more sovereignly indifferent, such as cancer, remains: "Der Mann, der am Krebs verendete, suchte mit allen Mitteln die Poesie dieses peinlichen Geschehnisses auf die Zunge zu kriegen, er malte sich Bilder vom Leid der Erde, die ihn ausspie, vom Schmerz der Hinterbleibenden oder der grandiosen und ihn ergreifenden Ironie ihrer Gleichgültigkeit und vom Dunkel, das ihn aufnahm" (GW, XX, 4–5). The point of view Brecht takes here is that of the dying man, that of Baal at the end, with the great question of the darkness ahead for the dying. Brecht views "God" as a desperate attempt of the dying to save themselves. After describing how all men, each according to his intelligence, have made ever more clever attempts to deceive themselves into believing that there is a God who saves from the darkness, Brecht, who is only too intimately involved in this question, concluded that all human efforts to invent a God are doomed to failure: "Als die wimmelnde Masse der Wesen auf dem fliegenden Stern sich kennengelernt und ihre unbegreifliche Verlassenheit empfunden hatte, hatte sie schwitzend Gott erfunden, den niemand sah, also daß keiner sagen konnte, es gäbe ihn nicht, er habe ihn nicht gesehen" (GW, XX, 5).

Brecht sees religion as man's terrified response, almost the response of a trapped animal, to his feeling of being totally abandoned in the universe that gave him birth (Verlassenheit will occur prominently in the plays we shall study) and to his uncontrollable fear of the oncoming darkness of death. These two feelings, and the concomitant problem of "being good" in such a world, are the key to Brecht's nonsatiric use of the Bible. The parts of the Bible that Brecht uses empathetically are those in which these two feelings, the feeling of being abandoned and the fear of death, as well as the problem of "being good," are most poignantly expressed. The other books of the Bible are either satirized, handled humorously, or ignored.

In the plays studied, Brecht's use of the Old Testament is heavily restricted to the Wisdom literature and Prophetic literature. Among the Wisdom writings Brecht leans most heavily on Ecclesiastes, Job, and the Psalms. These books are most congenial to Brecht since they too, like most of the Old Testament, operate under the assumption that there is no real afterlife (no *Jenseits*) for man, and have a dominating awareness of death and abandonment, unrelieved by their belief in God and His immortality.

In Prophetic literature, especially Isaiah, the problem of being good among men and of exposing the phenomenon of religion's ignoring of social injustice while paying careful attention to the performance of ritual, is the whole burden of the message. Here also there is no real belief in things being "fixed up" after death for the poor and the oppressed, "the widow, the orphan, the resident alien," and so the religious man must help them now, since—as Brecht would say— "[Wir] können einem toten Mann nicht helfen" (GW, II, 564).

Although Brecht may parody almost any well-known verse or verses from the New Testament, especially moral ones, for achieving humor or satire, he also makes empathetic use of the the New Testament. But his use is almost totally restricted to the events of the Passion and Death accounts, especially St. Matthew's Passion. The Resurrection accounts are never used.

Thus we return to Mayer's original observation, "Blasphemie, Anspielung, Verfremdung. Trotzdem ist da noch mehr." This "noch mehr" I have found to be primarily located in a line of plays which begins with *Die Bibel* and culminates in *Mutter Courage*. The plays in this line are characterized by the use of some variation of the "city" or "besieged city" motif, there is no "happy end," and the hero or heroine is ultimately confronted with abandonment and death in a way that is evocative of the Crucifixion.

By contrast, Brecht's use of the Bible, in other plays with apparent religious themes, such as *Leben des Galilei*, in which there is no serious confrontation with death, rarely go beyond the realm of argumentation and dialectics and seldom exceed the extent that one finds even in *Baal*. The same is true for plays occupied with socio-moral questions rather than the life-death question, such as *Der gute Mensch von Sezuan* and *Der kaukasische Kreidekreis*. Concerning these plays, I am in general agreement with Grimm's modified analysis of Brecht's use of the Bible. Only in his tragedies of abandonment and death does

Brecht, it seems, go beyond the level of "blasphemy, allusion, and alienation" that Grimm believes to be typical of Brecht's general use of the Bible.

In order to show that there is a fundamental affinity of thought between Brecht and certain authors and parts of the Bible on the question of death and human goodness, an affinity that did not change in the course of time, I have tried to trace the persistence of these patterns over long periods of Brecht's life. For this reason I have selected four plays for detailed analysis that are widely separated chronologically (the reader can easily extrapolate to others). Except for *Die Bibel*, the plays are approximately ten years apart. Since each play deals with some tragic aspect of "the city," both change and persistence of attitude on the part of Brecht can be easily seen. The four plays are *Die Bibel* (1914), "the city besieged"; *Baal* (1918), from the early jubilantly nihilist period because it so clearly revels in death's long siege of life; *Mahagonny* (1927–29), from his period of transition to communism; and *Mutter Courage* (1938–39), from his later, mature period.

The backbone of each chapter is an "outline commentary," which I hope will be a convenient help for the reader, and which I hope will help even the more skeptical not to laugh except perhaps in recognition. "Sie werden lachen: die Bibel."[25]

II

Die Bibel: The City Besieged

To someone aware of the great importance of the Bible and of biblical thought in the later works of Bertolt Brecht, it comes as a somewhat pleasant confirmation to discover that the first play completed by Brecht bears the resoundingly simple title: *Die Bibel*.[1] One can scarcely underestimate the surprising richness and the fundamental importance of *Die Bibel* for a thorough understanding of Brecht's writing.[2]

The basic situation of the city surrounded by an attacking army, or rather the basic situation of a Protestant city besieged by an attacking army of Catholics, with which we are so familiar from the concluding scenes of *Mutter Courage* and from the initial scenes of the *Augsburger Kreidekreis* and *Der kaukasische Kreidekreis*, appears here in its first and primeval form. One is so amazed by its fundamental similarity to the later plays as to come to doubt the now sacred theories of the necessary evolution of a writer's thought. Perhaps it is a good reminder to us that even in evolution there is something that remains, a fundamental thing that is always there, that is constantly being unfolded in different forms.

The play is divided into three scenes. In the first, the grandfather and the young girl are together in a comfortable middle-class living room; in the background there is the noise of battle; in the foreground the grandfather is reading from the Bible. In the second scene, the father, who is burgomaster of the town, enters with his son. The crisis is begun and ended as the father tells the grandfather the terms under which the Catholics will accept a surrender of the town: conversion of the inhabitants, and the sending out of the burgomaster's daughter to the tent of the Catholic general. The girl decides not to go but to remain with the upright and righteous grandfather. In the third scene, the daughter and the grandfather are once again alone with themselves and their Bible, as fire and destruction rain down on house and town.

The plot is in no way complicated and reflects certain commonplaces of Brechtian style. The use of the Bible, the use of the besieged city as a catalyst for moral crisis, the *Verfremdung* of the official importance of war by juxtaposing it to the seemingly small problems of the human individual, and relegating it to the realm of background while the "little" problems take up the foreground; Brecht's fundamental sympathy with human weakness, moral frailty, and his rejection, with grudging respect, of human strength and moral righteousness.

The theme of the play is best seen in the conflict between the grandfather and the father in the second scene—a conflict set in the biblical terms of the apocryphal book of Judith. The inhabitants must acknowledge the faith of the investing army, and there is a girl who goes out to the enemy general. Brecht, of course, changes the story to fit his theme. In *Die Bibel* the Protestant girl ends up hesitating to go to the Catholic Holofernes, and thereby brings about the destruction of the city rather than the salvation of it.

The father, the burgomaster of the town, is the person caught in the moral conflict. It is he who is made to stammer as he states the two conditions set by the Catholic army to the righteous grandfather, and who hears himself condemned by his own father for even considering giving over his daughter. In this scene the grandfather and the brother are depicted as absolutists, the characters with strong positions. The father, the morally wavering and weak human being, is the character of love and not of sureness.

On the one hand, the brother, the soldier, keeps saying with a more-than-Kantian moral imperative: "Mädchen, ich sage dir, du mußt! . . . Ein Volk schreit nach dem Opfer!" (It seems unnecessary to give page citations for each quotation from *Die Bibel*, since the play is quite short and is entirely contained in eight pages [GW, VII, 3031–3038]). He even tempts her with the thought of saving the family and kin: "Du rettest ein Volk! Ein Volk! Du rettest deine Verwandten. Deinen Vater! Deinen Großvater!" On the other hand, the grandfather maintains the absolute biblical imperative not to betray God: "Eine Seele ist mehr wert als 1000 Körper," he says, implying in no uncertain terms that the sinful offering of her body to the general would in no way please God. He denies the moral validity of saving the family and relatives through immoral conduct by approximately citing one of the more severe passages from the New Testament: "Wer mich verleugnet vor den Menschen, den will auch ich verleugnen vor dem himmlischen Vater! . . . Wahrlich, sagt der Herr, wer Vater oder Mutter mehr lieb hat als mich, ist meiner nicht wert! — Du mußt fest bleiben, denk an deine Seele" (Mt 10:37). The brother attempts again to appeal to her heart and says to the grandfather and to his sister: "Schweig, du alter Narr! Mit deiner Bibel, die so kalt und gerecht ist, wie du! Folge deinem Herzen, Mädchen! Ist es nicht schön, für Tausende zu leiden?"

This type of debate, using two divergent systems of absolutes, is something that will be seen in practically all of Brecht's later plays, including another masterful debate of opposed biblical quotations, in *Leben des Galilei*. Here it is used to expose the overdemandingness both of righteous reading of the Bible and of sentimental idealism. Both brother and grandfather want to force the girl to do what they think is right. The father, who is caught in the middle, who out of weakness and sympathy for the multitude has actually thought of giving over his daughter, regardless of whether or not he thinks it is the right thing to do, suddenly becomes the focus of the play.

As opposed to the "du mußt's" of both sides, he suddenly intervenes with: "Laß sie! Zwing sie nicht!" He is not willing to force her into any action that she felt she could not do. He is the only one who accepted her original answer of "Ich kann's nicht tun" with a quietly resigned and fatherly: "Ich wußte es." Now he speaks again, not to debate which course of action is the morally superior one, but to affirm it to be her choice to decide, and to defend her freedom and the finality of her decision. At this point the theme of the play is stated simply and powerfully as the son tells the father what he is: "Du Schwächling!" Yet it is the father, the "weakling," whom Brecht, the fifteen-year-old author, defends. The absolutism of the son is made to seem foolish by his naive assumption that suffering is something wonderful: "Ist es nicht *schön*, für Tausende zu leiden?" The absolutism of the grandfather makes him feel no loving sympathy for the persons he is judging and makes him very selective in what he finds appealing in the Bible. He quickly leafs through the unappealing passages which state: "dienet eurem Nächsten . . . habt Mitleid mit dem, der da darbet" (Lk 10:27 ff.).

In his humane weakness the father possesses real hidden strength: "Junge! Laß ab von ihr! Ich befehl es!" And then comes the strange allusion to the beginning of the Passion of Christ, put into the mouth of the father. "Es ist genug." This allusion to the end of the Agony in the Garden and the coming of the soldiers for the beginning of the Passion and Death serves to put us in sympathy with the father, who will now be condemned by the righteous grandfather. "Du hast deiner Tochter Seele verschachern wollen. Hinaus mit dir! Du bist nicht wert, deine Tochter zu sehen." Is it possible to use Christ against the Bible? To bring the Protestant Bible to bear against Christianity? One of Brecht's more powerful *Verfremdungseffekte*,[3] I maintain, is to do precisely that. Christianity has grown so absolutist, and its interpretation of itself and its Scriptures has grown so absolutist, that were Christ to return he would probably be condemned by both Catholic and Protestant alike for being too "weak." This position, best known from Dostoevskii's masterful exposition of the three temptations of

Christ in the Grand Inquisitor scene in *The Brothers Karamazov*,[4] is
also a theme of the young Brecht. Moreover, if one looks ahead to the
condemnation to death of other "weak" characters such as Paul
Ackermann (Jimmy Mahonney) and Kattrin, one sees that they are
surrounded by the mature Brecht with the same Christ aura at the
moment of their death—usually by the same means as used here, a
simple allusion to one of Christ's statements made during the Passion.
The agony and passion of the father begin here too. Especially since
he accepts his father's judgment as accurate, and feels that he has
done wrong in even contemplating letting his daughter go to the
enemy general if she had so desired. "Ich bin's nicht wert . . . Ihr
habt recht . . . Ich bin's nicht wert . . . *Wankt hinaus.*"

By setting the father in this way in opposition to the grandfather,
Brecht is able to exercise a critique of the grandfather's Bible by the
only source whose criticism the grandfather and the Christian audience would have to take with ultimate seriousness: Christ. He places
the absolute moral imperatives of the New Testament in opposition to
the humane demands of the Passion and Death accounts of the New
Testament—thus forcing the audience to think more deeply about the
biblical clichés taken so long for granted.

Scene 2, which we have just considered, is structurally the middle
of the play. It is surrounded on both sides by scenes of war. The first
scene and the last scene set up what will again be seen in *Mutter
Courage* twenty-five years later: war seen as the fundamental metaphor for the moral environment of human life, for the human condition. The moral conflicts of individuals, though interesting and important to Brecht, are always seen in the perspective of a larger scene
in which they mean almost nothing, and this nemesis aspect of
tragedy is already present in *Die Bibel*.

The first scene of *Die Bibel* opens with war, but a very special type
of war, the war of Catholics against Protestants, a contradictory war
of two types of absolutists who, ironically enough, follow someone
who died rather than let Peter raise a sword against his enemies. This
exposure of the self-alienation of Christianity into two "warring"
groups and its infidelity to the dying Christ is the powerful opening
of *Die Bibel*. "Das Drama spielt in den Niederlanden, in einer von den
Katholiken belagerten protestantischen Stadt." This instruction is followed immediately by the words of Jesus on the cross, read by the
grandfather:

Und um die neunte Stunde rief Jesus laut und sprach: "Mein Gott, mein
Gott, warum hast du mich verlassen," and nach einer Weile spotteten die um
ihn standen und sagten: Anderen hat er geholfen, aber sich selbst kann er

nicht helfen. Steig herab vom Kreuz und wir wollen Dir glauben. Da schrie Jesus abermals: "Es ist vollbracht" und neigte das Haupt und verschied.

I conceive of much of the play as a meditation on this section of the Passion. The abandonment of Christ by God is something that will be felt by the audience in the condition of the father as cruelly proclaimed by the grandfather. The weakness of Christ, which caused him to be exposed to the mockery of the "strong" who were not crucified, results in the ancient challenge of the "strong": "Come down from the cross and we will believe in you." Christ also dies and disappears from the scene and leaves life to go on, run by the "strong." Brecht will always have a scene following the death of such characters as his Father, Baal, Kattrin, and Paul Ackermann, showing the continuation of the human condition regardless of the efforts of the "good."

The part of the passage above that seems most important to Brecht, however, is "Anderen hat er geholfen, aber sich selbst kann er nicht helfen." This theme of not being able to help, is repeated in the same scene. The grandfather reemphasizes it when he says: "Heute ist ein schwerer Tag. Der Feind will stürmen. Wir sind hier und können nicht helfen. Wir können nur Gott um Hilfe bitten. Laßt uns beten! Wir wollen Trost suchen in der Bibel."

Here is perhaps the first and basic place where Brecht broaches the metaphysical problem of the real possibility of helping: risking self in order to render personal aid. Does help accomplish anything if it is in the face of death? Later this question will reach astonishing proportions and lead to despair in *Mahagonny*, where Weill's music will make helplessness the unforgettable chant at the end of the play— "Können uns und euch und niemand helfen!" In *Mutter Courage*, the peasants will use the same logic as the grandfather does here to excuse their doing nothing as the Catholics sneak up for an attack on the city. They too will conclude that the only thing they can do without threatening themselves is to pray.

This "not being able to help," however, which the son mistakes for weakness, as do the crucifiers of Christ, is actually the goodness of the father, who will not force his daughter, and leaves her free to do what she thinks is right. This is opposed to the decisive "strength" of the Catholics, who are willing to burn down cities to force others to accept Christ as they see him, and the "strength" of the grandfather, who is willing to see thousands burn rather than let one night of extramarital sex break Christ's "unforgiving" moral code. The grandfather, too, shows the same almost frivolous naiveté toward the Bible as the son does to his code of the heart, when he praises the Bible for being "wonderful." "Dieses Buch ist so schön. Weil es stark ist." The grandfather also manages to distance himself from humanity by adding, as if he were not a human, "Die Menschen sollten es mehr lesen."

In this scene the daughter is kept somewhat in a Gretchen role. She is not made into a semiheroic Judith, but is more an innocent pawn—as will be the case with Kattrin up until the end, when she suddenly turns and warns the city. The daughter in *Die Bibel* is simply made to allude to Gretchen with her essentially repeated line, "Es ist so seltsam schwül hier."[5]

In the third and last scene, the father is gone. The grandfather and the daughter are alone again in the room as in the first scene. The scene is begun very humanly as both daughter and grandfather reflect on the hardness with which he dealt with the father. Death is brought in as the girl reflects on the death of the mother and the love which the father bore her through the mother. Then comes the apocalypse. In a scene that reminds one of the end of Kaiser's *Gas* trilogy, fire and thunderous explosions put an end to the play. The church bells ring to warn of the end, and the God of the Grandfather is there in judgment.

The last scene is the Day of Judgment promised in the first scene, where allusion had been made to the Eschatological Discourse in Mark 13, on the destruction of the city of Jerusalem. The grandfather says in the first scene: "Wenn aber solche Zeichen geschehen, müßt ihr auf die Berge fliehen! Seid standhaft dann und treu. Denn es hängt davon viel ab!" This same scene is also, however, made by Brecht into the hour of Crucifixion. In the first speech of the play the very first words spoken were: "Und um die neunte Stunde. . . ." This hour is still honored in many Catholic countries by keeping total silence each year on Good Friday from noon until 3:00 p.m. Thus the hour of three o'clock is probably the only time that is popularly known of the different "hours" mentioned in the New Testament. Brecht is able to use this tradition as a way to bind the first and last scenes around the middle one. In the first scene the hour of the crucifixion is mentioned: "Um die neunte Stunde"; in the second scene, the brother announces the time of the final attack: "Und heut, jetzt dann, um 3 Uhr, beginnt der große Sturm. Der Katholik stürmt." Later in the second scene, the brother warns about the approaching three o'clock: "Haha! *Plötzlich abbrechend, da die Uhr zweimal schlägt.* Schon ½ auf 3 Uhr! Mädchen! Komm! 3 Uhr ist die letzte Frist." Then finally in the third scene the build-up comes to a climax as the *Sturmglocken* ring in three o'clock, the ninth hour.

The ending of the third scene expresses the horror of the two absolutist forces as they encounter each other, the loud roaring of the Catholic cannons and Catholic flames bursting around the house with the reply of the resounding Protestant church bells and the shouted defiance of the grandfather: "Gott ist mit uns!" Not only is "Gott mit uns" one of the "holy war" mottoes of Israel—as well as the messianic hope of Isaiah 7:14—but it is also the motto of Imperial Germany. Brecht here is attacking both the religious presumptuousness of "holy war" and the dangerous presumption of the Kaiser to be able to wage it "with God on our side."

The last line of the play strikes a somewhat more compassionate note. In his ninth-hour triumphal cry, "Gott ist mit uns," the grandfather contradicts the abandonment by God cited in the first speech of the play through the first words Jesus spoke at his ninth hour, "mein Gott, mein Gott, warum hast du mich verlassen?", a religious sentiment which would seem to make humility rather than holy war the only possible consequence. Then, however, as the house is going up in flames, the tone changes from that of motto and assurance that God is with us, to that of the prayer of the disciples on the way to Emmaus when they were afraid, for the first time, that he who was with them might now be leaving them, "Herr, bleibe bei uns, denn es will Abend werden und der Tag hat sich geneiget" (Lk 24:19).

A masterful handling of the Bible—and by a fifteen-year old! If the reader will examine the outline commentary on *Die Bibel* (pp. 20–22), he or she will be able to see the aesthetic and moral use to which Brecht puts the Bible. He estranges biblical statements by putting them into a new context so as to bring one to a greater enlightenment as to their meaning; the "es will Abend werden" of the Emmaus story, for example, refers to the evening of the death of a city. He also uses the Bible to set up a serious *casus moralis*: Is it more important to save a people: "Du rettest ein Volk," or for one individual to keep his uprightness: "Eine Seele ist mehr wert als 1000 Körper"; "Wer Vater oder Mutter mehr lieb hat als mich, . . ."? He thereby adds a strange depth to a short play that otherwise might be a case of family versus the welfare of the community. Brecht also at this early age is already using his technique of semi-biblical *Nachdichtung*, in one case to expose the contradictoriness of certain biblical imperatives by juxtaposing them to one another: "Wenn aber solche Zeichen geschehen, müßt ihr auf die Berge fliehen. Seid standhaft dann und treu." His technique includes adapting the texts slightly so as to make them more sharply contradictory, and of freely synthesizing a biblical teaching without bothering to quote exactly, but always being careful to use biblical German: "Ich aber sage euch, dienet eurem Nächsten! Brecht [!] dem Hungrigen das Brot und habt Mitleid. . . ." He also

creates a shock effect by changing only one word in a familiar quotation. For example, the well-known *verharr in deiner Sünde* becomes in
Brechtian German as the brother speaks to the grandfather: "Ja, verharr' nur . . . in deiner starren Gerechtigkeit!" In all of this, however,
there emerges a pattern that we will attempt to show as existing in
the later plays as well: a new hermeneutic of the Passion and Death
accounts of the New Testament.

In *Die Bibel* the identification of the hero with the Passion and
Death of Christ is used to gain sympathy (not at all *Verfremdung*) for
human weakness, human frailty. Most of the places referred to in the
above paragraph are *loci* where Brecht uses the technique of *Verfremdung* of a known (usually moralizing) text in order to get distance
from it so as to take intelligent issue with it, or get some insight into
its real implications. It is my contention, however, that where he uses
the Passion and Death accounts, they are used for the opposite purpose: to gain sympathy and empathy for the weak, "good" person.

Table 1

Die Bibel	Biblical Correlative
Sc. 1: A city; Protestant, besieged by Catholics	In Judith, a surrounded city; enemy believes in another god (same situation in *Mutter Courage*).
Um die neunte Stunde . . . Mein Gott, Mein Gott, warum hast du mich verlassen	Mt 27:46 (& Mk) Crucifixion.
Anderen hat er geholfen, aber sich selbst kann er nicht helfen. Steig herab vom Kreuz . . . Da schrie Jesus abermals Es ist vollbracht	Mt 27:42 Crucifixion; theme of *Mahagonny*. Mt 27:40 cf. Kattrin's death. Lk 23:46. Jn 19:30 Crucifixion: cf. soldier's statement at Kattrin's death: "Sie hats geschafft."
. . . neigte das Haupt und verschied.	Jn 19:30 Crucifixion.
Wir sind hier und können nicht helfen. (Großvater)	continuation of "nicht helfen" theme from above; cf. *Mahagonny* ending and attitude of peasant in *Mutter Courage*, Scene 11.

Table 1 *(continued)*

Wenn aber solche Zeichen geschehen, müßt ihr auf die Berge fliehen! Seid standhaft dann und treu. Denn es hängt davon viel ab!	Mk 13:4–8 and 13:14b and 13:13b (adapted: Wer. . . ausharrt; left out: wird gerettet werden!) and es hängt . . .-Brecht. Taken from the Eschatological Discourse on the destruction of Jerusalem and the End.
Ich aber sage euch, dienet eurem Nächsten! Brecht dem Hungrigen das Brot und habt Mitleid. . . . *Blättert.*	biblical *Nachdichtung*, a Brechtian synthesis of New Testament social teaching based on Lk 10:27 ff.
Wer Vater oder Mutter mehr liebt denn mich, der ist meiner nicht wert.	Mt 10:37.
Sc. 2: Wenn . . . ein Mädchen sich opfere . . . dem feindlichen Feldherr . . . eine Nacht	Judith 7:30–14:10, except that Judith had no relations with Holofernes, and Brecht's Protestant Judith refuses to go.
Du rettest ein Volk versus Eine Seele ist mehr wert als 1000 Körper!	Judith in the Old Testament versus popular Christian tradition (a distortion, perhaps, of "one lost sheep found is worth 99 that are safe").
Wenn der Tag des Gerichtes kommt, wie wirst du dastehen?	popular preaching tradition.
Hab Erbarmen, Mädchen, mit den Tausenden!	Mt 14:14; Mk 1:1; Jn 6—the feeding of the five thousand.
3 Uhr ist die letzte Frist.	3 Uhr = the ninth hour (cf. Scene 1) the hour of Death in the Crucifixion.
Ja, verharr' nur . . . in deiner starren Gerechtigkeit!	possibly Mk 16:16 or Jn 20:23. The normal expression is *in seiner Sünde verharren.*

Table 1 *(continued)*

Wer mich verleugnet vor den Menschen, den will auch ich verleugnen vor dem himmlischen Vater!	Mt 10:33
Wer Vater oder Mutter mehr lieb hat als mich, . . .	Mt 10:37.
Tag des Gerichtes . . . gerecht!	Mt 25:31 ff.
Es ist genug. (Vater)	Mk 14:41 end of the Agony in the Garden, beginning of the Passion and Death.
Sc. 3: Sei gnädig Gott ist mit uns	prayer formulation. "Emmanuel"; Is 7:14, but used here in a general Old Testament holy-war context, alluding to the Kaiser's motto.
Destruction of the city by fire	Day of Judgment, by fire: popular Christian tradition; destruction of Jerusalem.
Herr, bleibe bei uns, denn es will Abend werden und der Tag hat sich geneiget.	Lk 24:29, Emmaus. Used here, however, in an apocalyptic sense rather than in the original Easter Sunday context.

It is appropriate to conclude with a comparison between Brecht's *Die Bibel* and the book of Judith from which the basic plot is taken.[6] In the book of Judith the idea of the salvation of the city of Bethulia, surrounded by the army of Nebuchadnezzar under Holofernes, is accomplished by Judith's going to the tent of Holofernes. She deliberately wears all her finery in order to entice him, and when she has, she waits until he has gotten himself drunk with wine, and then cuts off his head with his own sword. She brings the head back to the surrounded city and has it hung from the battlements. When the Assyrians see it in the morning, they run in panic as the Israelites attack from the city. The theology of Judith is one that reflects a unique attitude to history and to the God of history. When the elders think of surrendering the city (and therefore bowing to the god of Holofernes,

Nebuchadnezzar) if the Lord does not send relief within a certain period of time, Judith accuses them of misunderstanding God, and of attempting to deal with him as if he were a man. She says God will send help if and when he pleases, or not at all if he so pleases. She then proceeds to make herself into the possible means of that help coming, by going out to slay Holofernes. She embodies the paradoxical but religious attitude of accepting that all comes unchangeably from God, and at the same time doing your best to bring about the changes you want to come!

Brecht has borrowed only the barest basic story and the general situation of a city under siege in a religious war, translating the city from Palestine to the Netherlands. He has attempted to switch the issue of whether or not the "good side" is going to win in the end to the issue of whether or not a little more human weakness might not be the solution—"immoral" though that may at first appear. If the daughter had gone to the Catholic general, as Judith did to the Assyrian, perhaps in this "immoral" way the Christian city would have been saved, as the Hebrew one was. But instead Christian righteousness does not permit this Old Testament solution, and leads instead to fire and destruction. The Old Testament belief that God works as much through evil as good, that the pagan Cyrus can be proclaimed by the prophet as the hand of God as much as the high priest in the temple, that the frailty of human beings may be as close or closer to the Divine (closer to the Divine Suffering Servant), than the strength of those who "need no physician," is an old insight that Brecht is perhaps trying to recover in this play about the ninth hour.

III

Baal: A Bohemian in the City

Four years after finishing *Die Bibel*, Brecht wrote another play with an almost as obviously biblical title: *Baal*. He was only twenty years of age and in many respects the play is that of a young man in revolt, but it once again displays a mastery of the use of biblical motifs with personal reinterpretation. The overall horizon and the thrust of this play are unashamedly pagan, and take it far beyond the moral-protest confines of *Die Bibel*. Sex, human cruelty, indifference, vulgarity and humor are placed within the cycle of nature and are accepted with their embodying god—Baal. The conflict of opposing armies, of opposing ideologies, or righteousness and idealism, give way to the conflict of life and death. *Baal* is a play of reaction and of assertion. Between the cataclysmic ending of *Die Bibel* and the writing of *Baal*, World War I had intervened. Martin Esslin, though perhaps insufficiently skeptical as to the extent of Brecht's war experience, writes:

In 1916 he [Brecht] left school and moved to Munich, where he began to read medicine and science at the university. But after a few terms he had to interrupt his studies. It was wartime and he was called up. Being a medical student, he became a medical orderly in a military hospital.
    There can be no doubt that this was one of the decisive events of his life.
    I was mobilized in the war [he told Sergei Tretyakov] and placed in a hospital. I dressed wounds, applied iodine, gave enemas, performed blood transfusions. If the doctor ordered me: "Amputate a leg, Brecht!" I would answer: "Yes, Your Excellency!" and cut off the leg. If I was told: "Make a trepanning!" I opened the man's skull and tinkered with his brains. I saw how they patched people up in order to ship them back to the front as soon as possible.
    Seeing human beings cut up in this way and having to do the gruesome work himself was a traumatic experience that left lasting traces in Brecht's character and work.[1]

One of the results of his seeing the senseless suffering of the soldiers in the military hospital would be his lifelong pacifism and his horror at the futility of war. An even more personal result, however, would be his seeing the human being as a "corpse on furlough," a complex of organic matter and hair, alive and vital, struggling against ultimately hopeless odds in striving to remain alive, not to be thrown into the river. Perhaps this experience of human mortality is traceable to his study of medicine. At about this same time he must first have assisted in the dissection of cadavers at the medical faculty in Munich. The immediacy of such an experience must have been reinforced immeasurably for the young Brecht by his having to see men die before him in the military hospital despite all their attempts to hold onto life. Seeing people go from various states of health and from being wounded to being a cadaver is the experience that is reflected in *Baal*. His amputations and trepannings must have made hm experience all the more directly and personally the frailty of the human person's body with removable limbs like those of a tree. In any case, it is awareness of human fragility that comes to be expressed in *Baal*, though the actual number of experiences in the military hospital must have been far less than Brecht claimed. Indeed Dieter Schmidt has shown that Brecht the poet and his followers deeply mythologized Brecht's rather scant military experience as an orderly in ward D (the venereal disease section) of the military hospital in Augsburg.[2] Brecht apparently did not always bother to show up in uniform and enjoyed himself composing bawdy songs for the soldiers. Still, despite the braggadocio, I think it is safe to assume that Brecht came to see more of what goes on in a hospital than the occasional entertainment he provided in ward D. And here also he may well have cast more than a furtive glance at corpses. Even Schmidt thinks Brecht was affected by his three months at the hospital and cites the "Ballad of the Dead Soldier." Despite his very proper skepticism about Brecht's "military service," Schmidt concludes: "Dennoch ist Brecht, trotz aller zur Schau getragenen Kaltschnäuzigkeit, empfindsam und verwundbar. Durch die vierteljährige Arbeit auf einer Lazarettstation, auf der er mit besonders widerwärtigen Krankheiten umgehen muß, ist er vom Krieg und seinen Begleiterscheinungen angeekelt."[3]

It is no longer the problem of human righteousness and absolutism that concerns him. He has found a new and more horrible absolute than the grandfather's righteousness: death. *Baal* is thus not a World-War-I plea for the stopping of useless killing (war does not occur in a single scene of the play) but rather it is the shock of the medical student amd military orderly who has discovered the weakness of the human organism, the frailty of human life, and the tenacity with which the dying hold on to it. He has discovered the transitory nature of human existence. It is this death-and-body-centered, biomedical concept of man that the student Brecht will use to refute the non-scientific, romantically-biblical glorification of man as poet, which is found in Hanns Johst's *Der Einsame*.

While *Baal* as a drama is far more than a *Gegenstück* to *Der Einsame*,
still the initial impulse for it came from a feeling of opposition to that
play,[4] and thus it is useful to find what in *Der Einsame* might have
sufficiently aroused the young author's ire that he would transfer it
into a play cast in the biblical mold of the pagan god opposed to the
God of Israel.

There is a speech that is one of the better in *Der Einsame*, but one
which probably would have annoyed the young Brecht—both because of its partial accuracy and because of its somewhat condescend-
ing tone. It is spoken by the intoxicated Grabbe about two young
medical students in the thick tobacco smoke of a *Schenkkeller*. It has
been an all-night affair, everyone has gone home except Grabbe and
his circle, and two anatomy students have just left that *in-vino-veritas*
group to say good night. Grabbe is speaking:

Sind liebe Jungen, die beiden Kleinen! Saufen wacker! Und sind keine
Dichter! Ich beneide immer diese Kerle. Unsereiner sieht in jedem Menschen
ein Märchen. Die sind praktischer!! Die schneiden einfach den Menschen
auf. Und finden ein Herz, tatsächlich in jedem Menschen ein gleiches Herz:
Und finden in jedem Menschen überhaupt die gleichen Dinge! Nur eben das
Märchen finden sie nicht, um das wir uns abquälen!— — —(Pause.) Ich hätte
sollen Mediziner werden! Da sieht man seine Arbeit.[5]

It is easy to see the poet who was filled with horror at the casualness
of "Amputate a leg, Brecht!" reacting strongly to the antibiological
facileness of "Die schneiden einfach den Menschen auf!" On the
other hand, Brecht as *poet* as well as medical student, knew both
sides of the problem that Johst is broaching here, and seems in *Baal* to
be more angered at the exclusive aestheticism of the question than at
the question. He will have the experience of the cut-up bodies and
the floating corpse in the river to oppose to Johst's Grabbe, deliberately describing the human body in a repulsively biological manner
in *Baal*. *Märchen* and myth gradually desert the decaying corpse in the
poem "Als sie ertrunken war":

> . . .
> Tang und Algen hielten sich an ihr ein
> So daß sie langsam viel schwerer ward
> Kühl die Fische schwammen an ihrem Bein:
> Pflanzen und Tiere beschwerten noch ihre letzte Fahrt.
> . . .
> Als ihr bleicher Leib im Wasser verfaulet war
> Geschah es, sehr langsam, daß Gott sie allmählich vergaß:
> Erst ihr Gesicht, dann die Hände und ganz zuletzt erst ihr
> Haar. (GW, I, 53)

There is, however, another element in *Der Einsame* that may have angered the writer of *Die Bibel*: Johst's use of the Bible. Johst depicts the artist-poet as the outcast within bourgeois society—a common enough theme, to be sure, handled far more ably by Thomas Mann and Hermann Hesse. Instead of leaving this situation of being an outcast as the state of the gifted among the nongifted, Johst uses the Bible to turn the drunken artist into a sort of Christ among the Pharisees. Still, like the hints of homosexuality that are used for titillation in the third scene (but which really are not more than the pun on *beischlafen* as said by Hans to Christian),[6] so also the comparisons made by Grabbe between himself and Christ are no more than linguistic. The play itself gives them no life-and-death seriousness, the sparse aestheticism of the text relegates them to the realm of small-minded presumptuousness. Whether this "chutzpah" should be chiefly attributed to Johst or to the character Grabbe is something I leave to the reader to decide; the play itself is what provoked Brecht's reaction. The following are the major biblical allusions used by Johst, in the order in which they occur in *Der Einsame*.

In accepting the death of his wife Grabbe says: "Das Gethsemane Jenes ist ein Jahrmarkt gegen dieses Gesetz, was sich hier alltäglich— ich weiß ja! alltäglich—erfüllt!" (p. 17).[7] To calm Grabbe's hysterical agony his friend Hans is made to put a drug into a cup filled with wine, a cup which is then called a chalice, as if, perhaps, cup were not obvious enough:

Hans: (hat in einen Becher ein Pulver geschüttet und reicht ihm den Becher mit Wein gefüllt) Nimm, Christian, und trinke, Christian!! Trink dir Schlaf, mein Christian!!
Christian: (sieht ihn verzweifelt durch und durch und faßt den Kelch mit beiden Händen) Das ist das Furchtbarste! . . . Jener trank aus dem Kelche den Tod und die Wahrheit. Wir aber saufen Schnaps . . . und verludertes Leben!! (pp. 17–18)

After sleeping with Hans's wife Isabella, Grabbe explains himself this way to Hans: "Du weißt, wer du mir bist! Ich habe einen Berg Horeb! Und ein Gesicht ins gelobte Land!" (p. 39). On receiving a notice from the civil court Grabbe says: "So also sieht mein König aus dem Morgenlande aus. Seltsame Anbetung!" (p. 46). To his mother as a plea for confidence in him when she tries to get him to do some work:

Grabbe: Der Sohn Marias wurde als Verbrecher ans Kreuz geschlagen, und Maria nahm ihn doch als den Sohn Gottes!—Und glaubte an ihn und sein Reich!—Und sein Reich kam!
Mutter: Versündige dich nur noch! So ist es recht! Frevel noch und Überhebung zu allem! (p. 50)
. . .

Grabbe: Wo nimmst du, Mutter, das Recht her, dich so zum Richter aufzu-
werfen? Daß du Windeln mir wuschest? (pp. 50–51)

To the owner of the Rathskeller trying to wake up the half-drunk
Grabbe: "Grabbe: Das Meer! Das Meer! . . . Wie kann er den Schlummer eines Gesalbten stören!?" (p. 58). To the assembled city fathers
and others in the Rathskeller who have asked him to recite a poem of
his for their amusement: "Grabbe: Meine Herren! Ihre Bitte ehrt
mich! . . . Selten wurde ein Prophet in seiner Vaterstadt gelten gelassen" (p. 59). In a bar: "Sage mir nichts gegen sie . . . Die Menschen! . . . (lacht und streichelt über den Tisch hin, als ob er eine Flut
besänftige)" (p. 66). Perhaps the most important scene for us here,
and one to which Brecht alludes in *Baal*, is the scene in which Grabbe
hears of the death of his mother. Once again, in a bar:

Waldmüller: Also lies, was du vorhin geschrieben hast . . .
Grabbe: (liest) Golgatha. Christus wird vom Kreuz genommen. Maria weint
in die Wunden.—Wie der Wind stöhnt, Waldmüller!—
Ein Israelit: (kommt) Das Heiligste im Tempel ist zerrissen!
Maria: (die Nägelmale küssend) So ists!
Der Israelit: Die Gräber bersten!
Magdalena: (tröstend) Gottes Sohn zieht ein, die Hölle zu besuchen und den
Tod!
Maria: Mir so schmerzvoll entrissen!
Soldat der römischen Leibwache: (zu seinem Gefährten) Vide: Mater dolo-
rosa!
(Pause)
Waldmüller: Weiter, Grabbe! . . . Nur weiter! . . . Ich bin soweit!!
Grabbe: (wendet das Blatt, von dem er las) Lies selbst!
Waldmüller: (nimmt und liest) Der Totenschein deiner Mutter!?
Grabbe: Es ist die Quittung auf ihren Tod.—Du hast recht! . . . —Man hat
sie heute auf dem Armenanger eingescharrt wie einen tollen Hund. Und statt
der Blumen hat ihr der Herr Pastor ein paar Flüche nachgeworfen über ihren
ungeratenen und verlorenen Sohn!! . . .
Waldmüller: (sich tief verneigend) Ecce: poeta dolorosus! (pp. 67–68)

It is curious also to note that the play ends with the words, "die
Stimme des Weltgerichts." The voice is associated, however, with the
music of Beethoven! "Als wäre es," the words that precede the
phrase on the Day of Judgment, might unfortunately be taken as the
motto for the whole of the play. Brecht will substitute his own version
of "eternal" music for the trumpets of Beethoven and it will, of
course, be the guitar of the street and cabaret. He will also take the
cold stars of the scientific heavens, investing them with only a very
questionable indication of any possibility of a *Jenseits*, the world beyond, and substitute them for Johst's stars, which are merely used as

a literary metaphor for human emotion. Johst has Grabbe say: "Tränen springen zur Welt und sind Sterne eines übermächtigen Himmels—eines ewigen Reiches!" (p. 10). Brecht has Baal say "Sterne . . . hm" (GW, I, 60). Johst's "wind" will react sympathetically to the description of Christ's crucifixion, Brecht's "wind" is the indifferent terrestrial atmosphere, the presence of death itself.

I think we can see here major differences between Brecht's use of the Bible and Johst's. In no case does Johst question a statement of the Bible by standing it on its head, or by putting it into a situation which will cause its meaning to be questioned rather than taken for granted. There is no dispute with the statement; rather it is strictly speaking, *used*, fitted into the plot sequence of a play about a poetic megalomaniac, to show his megalomania, and to side with it. One can contrast this with the tension between text and action in *Die Bibel*: "Brecht dem Hungrigen das Brot und habt Mitleid . . . *Blättert*," or within the text as in "Wenn aber solche Zeichen geschehen, müßt ihr auf die Berge fliehen! Seid standhaft und treu." (Cf. pp. 18 and 21 above.) Even more can one think of the *context* into which the first words of *Die Bibel* are put ("Mein Gott, mein Gott, warum hast du mich verlassen?"): an attack by Christ's followers on a city of another group of Christ's followers.

Theologically one might say Johst uses Scripture incarnationally and not eschatologically. The poet is referred to, even if ironically, as "the Anointed." The poet's sleep in a bar is the "Schlummer eines Gesalbten" (Mk 4:38). He was wrapped in "winding clothes" (Lk 2:7) by his mother and is brought letters by "magi from the East" (Mt 2:1–12). He calms waters (Mk 4:39) and calls on his mother to believe in the "coming of his kingdom" (Lk 17:20–21). All of this emphasizes the poet's view of himself as another incarnate God. He is a person afflicted with the view that his surrounding world unfortunately does not recognize the divine in him—except perhaps when they are bored in the *Rathskeller* and call upon him and his poems for diversion. Even then he says, "Selten wurde ein Prophet in seiner Vaterstadt gelten gelassen." The poet Grabbe is described as sufficiently deluded as to view the death of his mother in terms of the death of Christ—thereby still keeping the attention and main glorification on himself. Composing poetry on the reverse side of the notification of his mother's death, he has an Israelite come and say that "the Most Holy in the temple has been torn apart." He then has Mary say, "It is so," while kissing the nail marks of her dead Son. The scene ends not with "Vide: Mater dolorosa!" but with "Ecce: poeta dolorosus!"

Brecht starts with the same problem of the poet outsider but removes the self-glorifying identification with the Anointed, and replaces it with a self-asserting identification with the anti-Judaeo-Christian god of fertility, Baal. The laziness of the poet will not be held at a distance by identifying it in the poet's mind with Jesus as a child being brought gifts, or with Jesus, the misunderstood prophet, or with Jesus, the hidden Divinity, the Christ; the laziness will be identified with the god of sensualism, Baal. The death of the poet will indeed be compared with the death of Christ, a death in abandonment rather than in a glorifying account of death with someone kissing the wounds: a death not accompanied by Beethoven played by students, but a death unaccompanied, and struggled against by an animal-like crawling across the floor to reach the door. The parts of the Passion and Death that will be brought in for identity will be the mocking and spitting in the face, "Could you not watch one hour with me," the feeling of "My God, why have you forsaken me?" as in *Die Bibel*, and not the Mater Dolorosa from the Pietà. Brecht will thus not totally reject a poetic identification of the dying hero with Christ, but insists on the unpleasant aspects of the tragedy of Christ's death.

To summarize: To Johst's Nature as reflecting man, Brecht opposes Nature as ignoring man; to Johst's elite aestheticism, a plebeian scientism; to Johst's intellectualism, animality; to his Jesus as the Anointed, Jesus as mocked; to the poet as another Christ, the poet as another Baal.

The conversion of the "Fall of the Anointed" into the "Fall of Baal" takes place in terms of the Baal myth. Brecht seems to have been quite familiar with the myth and to have made use of almost all of its traditional elements in *Baal*.[8] It is known that at this time he kept in his room both a skull and a picture of the Syrian god Baal over his bed: "Bei Brecht lag auf dem Tisch ein Totenschädel. . . . Über dem Bett hing, von seinem Schulfreund Caspar Neher gemalt, das Bild des syrischen Erdgottes Baal. Für Brecht war dieser Erdgott, den er seiner gleichnamigen Dramenfigur einverleibt hatte, die Verkörperung einer Unersättlichkeit nach Leben und einer ganz diesseitigen Lebensfrömmigkeit eigener Art."[9]

The worship of Baal predated the coming of the Hebrews into the land of Israel and continued successfully in the land during most of the time of the Old Testament despite constant tirades in almost every era against going up to the Canaanite "high places" and participating in the worship of the Baalim.

The worship of fertility is connected with the maintaining of life itself, and its continuation in time despite the death of each individual plant, animal and person. In the lands of the fertile crescent, bordering on the desert, this fertility is connected in a very intimate way with the presence of water as the source of life, and with rain as the bringer of water. Baal thus is depicted as the coming rain, the storm god, the weather god. In the famous illustration of the god Baal from the Ras Shamra stele in the Louvre, he is depicted as striding forward in the manner of an Egyptian god, a shaft of lightning in one hand, an upraised thunder-club in the other. Beneath him is a stylized representation of the mountaintops over which he strides (on which he is worshiped) and on his head is a crown composed of the two horns of the bull (the bull and the calf being the fertility animals connected with the cult), topped by a large phallus. The two long curling locks of hair may represent the clouds of the storm, as well as testes. Beneath the whole is a second wavy line which may represent the waters beneath the earth, source of life, replenished by the coming of Baal. In the ancient Ugaritic Krt epic we find lines not unlike many from Brecht's *Baal*:

> To the earth Baal rained
> To the field rained 'Aliy. [God]
> Sweet to the earth was Baal's rain
> To the field the rain of 'Aliy.[10]

In the play, Brecht makes almost constant use of rain as the background for almost all Baal scenes, and identifies Baal with calves and steers. More important will be the constant use of sex, which was the essential element in the worship of Baal, as is known from the denunciations of the prophets in the Bible.

The prophets Hosea and Isaiah both decry the sexual practices involved in the worship of Baal, which run the gamut from sacred ritual prostitution to copulation with animals. (It is curious that Brecht seems to have been so familiar with this whole tradition as to have Baal decry the impossibility of intercourse with trees.) Isaiah thunders:

Und ihr, kommt herzu, ihr Kinder der Tagwählerin, ihr Samen des Ehebrechers und der Hure. An wem wollt ihr nun eure Lust haben? Über wen wollt ihr nun das Maul aufsperren, und die Zunge herausrecken? Seid ihr nicht die Kinder der Übertretung, und ein falscher Same, die ihr in der Brunst zu den Götzen laufet unter alle grüne Bäume? . . . (Is 57:1–5)

Isaiah also alludes to the intercourse on the mountaintops and has God condemn it in no uncertain terms as an idolatrous adultery that breaks his compact with Israel. Isaiah complains of the phallic symbols that are set up in the houses so that the god of fertility will remember them (in Luther's German they are called *Gedächtnisse*): "Du machst dein Lager auf einen hohen erhabenen Berg, und gehest

daselbst auch hinauf zu opfern. Und hinter der Thür und Pfosten
stellst du dein Gedächtnis. Denn du wälzest dich von mir, und
gehest hinauf, und machest dein Lager weit, und verbindest dich mit
ihnen; du liebst ihr Lager, so du sie ersiehest" (Is 57:7–8).

In the same chapter Isaiah uses his main threat against the people
who worship in the nature and fertility cults of Baal. He uses the
main image for death and futility from the Wisdom tradition: the
wind. "Aber *der Wind* wird sie alle wegführen, und *Eitelkeit* wird sie
wegnehmen." In *Baal* Brecht uses this image to express the same
ultimate threat against life and life forces. Despite this threat,
however, and perhaps due to it, in accordance with the myth of the
annual death and resuscitation of life, the practice of ritual intercourse with Baal always continued. A Jesuit Scripture scholar comments:

> The myth of the death and resurrection of Baal represents the annual cycle of
> the cessation and return of fertility; by the ritual reenactment of the myth, the
> recurrence of the cycle is assured. . . . The ritual enactment of the myth no
> doubt included the sexual union of Baal and his consort, represented by a
> priest and a priestess, and sexual union of the worshipers with the goddess
> represented by the sacred prostitutes; by this sexual union they participated
> in the divine power of fertility.[11]

Apparently the blessings of the coming of fertility were also extended
to the animal kingdom by the devotees of Baal. The prophet Hosea
makes fun of those who kiss calves; he also warns them that they will
pass away like the morning dew: "Noch predigen sie von denselben:
wer die Kälber küssen will, der soll Menschen opfern [human
sacrifice and infanticide were also a part of the cult]. Die selbigen
werden haben die Morgenwolke und den Thau, der frühe fällt. Ja,
wie die Spreu, die von der Tenne verweht wird, und wie der Rauch
von der Feuermauer" (Hosea 13:2–3).

In addition to the sacredness of human intercourse with Baal and
intercourse between Baal and the calves, both of which Brecht seems
to have been quite aware of in *Baal*, trees are the third important
element in the cult. We have already seen Isaiah's complaint about
the people running in heat to worship the Baalim "under every green
tree." In Hosea there is a reference to the sacredness of the tree to
Baal worship and specifically the fig tree as being the sign of life in the
cult. Hosea has God say: "Nun will ich ihre Schande aufdecken vor
den Augen ihrer Buhlen, und niemand soll sie von meiner Hand
erretten. . . . Ich will ihre Weinstöcke und Feigenbäume wüste
machen, weil sie sagt: Das ist mein Lohn, den mir meine Buhlen
geben. Ich will einen Wald daraus machen, daß es die wilden Thiere

fressen sollen. Also will ich heimsuchen über sie die Tage Baalim . . ."
(Hosea 2:10–13). Since both vineyards and fig trees are regarded as
being given to the prostitute Israel by her lover Baal, it is assumed
they were connected with the cult. Brecht seems to have rendered the
sexual fertility connotation of "fig" extremely accurately into German
by the vulgar usage of "Pflaume" (vagina).[12] I believe this accounts
for the constant presence of not just trees in the sexual scenes but also
of the "Grüne Felder, blaue Pflaumenbäume" in Scene 8 and in other
scenes of hetero- or homosexuality, such as the April background to
Scene 4. The fig tree itself was, apparently, not only a sign of recur-
ring life, but also of sexuality and of the god Baal, and thus the proper
place under which to practice the sexual worship of the same god.
Phallic pillars, one of which is mentioned as being in the temple (2
Kings 23: 4 & 6–7) were also connected with the worship, but it seems
that Brecht made no use of this in the play. He used the tree symbol
instead, since he was concerned far more with the paradox that there
are those who *live* by *felling* trees. This brings us to the myth itself.

Most important for understanding Baal and *Baal* is a knowledge of
the myth and what it identifies as the enemy of Baal. The enemy of
Baal is Mat or Mot (death). Of all the gods, Baal is the only one who
does not have a house of his own—for a weather god this is under-
standable! He finally gets permission from El, the father of the gods,
to build one, and he builds it on top of a mountin, Mt. Sapan. This
insures that Baal will be content and will give his rain in due season.
After a battle with the sea (Yamm), Baal has a window installed in his
heavenly home.

Through the window, a cleft in the clouds, Baal gave forth his holy voice
which convulsed the earth and sent his enemies scurrying to the hills and
woods [thunder]. Issuing a challenge to his enemy Mot (death), who
presumed to rule gods and men, Baal dispatched his messengers to Mot's
infernal, filthy abode, warning them not to get close to Mot's rapacious jaws.

The sequel to this action is furnished by a group of texts which recount
Baal's confrontation with Mot. In his first encounter, Baal is invited to a
banquet at which he is to be both guest and main course. Baal's response to
Mot's invitation is abject surrender : "Thy slave am I; thine eternal." Before
descending to the realm of death, Baal copulates with a heifer [cult] and
begets a male offspring. After a textual gap, there is a report that Baal's
corpse has been found. El and Anath [Baal's sister and consort] mourn
violently.[13]

Baal's sister-consort Anath demanded that Mot release her brother. Mot
refused and boasted how he had mangled Baal. Anath then dismembered
Mot, scattered and burned the pieces, and gave them to the birds. Baal's
resurrection followed Mot's demise, the good news being transmitted
through a dream of El:

In a dream of Beneficent El Benign
A vision of the Creator of Creatures.
The skies rained oil,
The wadies flowed with honey.
So I knew that Mighty Baal lives,
The Prince, Lord of Earth, lives.

The fields were still parched from the drought and again Anath and Shapsh [the sun] set out to find Baal. Next both Mot and Baal appear reconstituted and reactivated and again in conflict. . . . Thus it is clear that Baal, representing the life-giving rains, fluctuates in his ability to withstand the power of Mot, who represents drought, sterility, and death.[14]

In addition to using the symbols of Baal in the play (rain, the calf and steer, the phallus, the tree) Brecht also used the annual time scale of the myth of Baal to counteract the time-ignoring myth of Grabbe. The play is stretched over a canvas of spring, summer, and fall, rather than across the non-natural background of *Der Einsame*, where there are no seasons and where the hero does not live or die in accord with them. In *Baal*, after the mention of the Flood and Noah, April is made the background for renewed sexual activity in Scene 4, *Baals Dach-kammer*, where it is connected with sex, smell, and the animals, as Baal says to Sophie: "Ich weiß es. Es ist der April. Es wird dunkel, und du riechst mich. So ist es bei den Tieren."[15] Naturally, the scene began by mentioning that it has been *raining* (p. 20), and when Sophie protests that she wants to be left alone, Baal protests: "Ich heiße Baal. . . . Du mußt mich trösten. Ich war schwach vom Winter. Und du siehst aus wie eine Frau" (p. 26). The scene ends with Baal saying, "Die Weiden am Fluß tropfnaß, vom Regen struppig. *Faßt sie*. Du mußt bleiche Schenkel haben" (p. 27). The interaction of rain, the animals, and sexual arousal within the general context of Baal's April rather than Grabbe's "poetry" is the biological-pagan answer to Johst's aesthetic-poetic explanation of sex. It also requires the careful use of the Baal myth in connection with the seasons.

In the second scene thereafter, *Mainacht unter Bäumen*, we have come to the beginning of summer, and the rain and fertility god speaks, naturally under a tree with Sophie, as Isaiah had decried: "Baal *faul*: Jetzt hat der Regen aufgehört. Das Gras muß noch naß sein . . . Durch unsere Blätter ging das Wasser nicht . . . Das junge Laub trieft vor Nässe, aber hier in den Wurzeln ist es trocken. *Bös*: Warum kann man nicht mit den Pflanzen schlafen?" (p. 29). Thus we reach May, or—as implied later in the scene where Sophie says that her mother has been thinking she has been dead since May (for about three weeks)—perhaps the beginning of June.

In the middle of the play there is a brief mention of the "Winterschlaf im schwarzen Schlamm für unsere weißen Leiber" (p. 42), and then it is mentioned in the midst of a sexual quarrel that it is Midsummer Day as Baal says to Sophie, "Geh zu den Flößern. Heut ist Johannis. Da sind sie besoffen" (p. 45). Then the trees of the succeeding scenes become less lush and gradually become northern. In Scene 16 hazel succeeds the lush green thickets of earlier scenes and the plum trees of even earlier scenes. Hazel gives way to *Ahorn im Wind* (maple in the wind) and as Baal's ever colder journal continues,—"Ich muß mich nach Norden halten" (p. 62)—following the "rib-side" of the leaves, he ends up, 10° Long. E. of Greenwich (which would presumably put him right back on the longitude of his beloved Black Forest), among those who kill trees, lumberjacks, and it is the second of November. It is both the end of autumn and Christianity's feast of the dead. Brecht puts it together in one word said by one of the rangers who is chasing Baal for his murder of Ekart, "Der schwarze Regen und dieser *Allerseelenwind*" (p. 63). It is in the next scene that Baal dies.

The other element from the Baal myth that Brecht used is the contest between life and death, Baal and Mot. The enemy of the poet is not misunderstanding on the part of bourgeois society, but the totally unfeeling Mot, the "wind," death itself. It is, of course, true that death is the enemy of all vegetation gods and life gods. To change Johst's theme from the artistic to the cosmic, any of the vegetative gods, including the classical Greek gods, might have been used as effectively by Brecht. Still, he gains something by way of a more absolute and metaphysical orientation by using the biblical god of vegetation (and, putatively, of evil) as the protagonist. He also assures himself of genuine, if antagonistic, involvement in the play by the contemporary Judaeo-Christian audience, to whom glorifying Pan or Bacchus is an acceptable and accustomed artistic endeavor. Glorifying Baal is not. Glorifying Baal strikes closer to home—and is far more guaranteed to achieve the effect of *épater le bourgeois*. Making death the antagonist demands the most serious struggle, since death exposes the most serious human weakness: mortality.

I do not think it is necessary to expose the underlying death images that pervade *Baal* in an exhaustive way. Let us simply take the basic life images from the Baal myth that Brecht uses and we can see that he has set up opposite images to them in order to depict the ancient struggle of Baal and Death. The life forces of "earth," "rain," and "tree," will be opposed by the naked "sky," the indifferent "stars," and the cold "wind." On the human level, human sexual love in the early and middle scenes will gradually be replaced by cold human indifference, especially on the part of the lumberjacks. Even the animals in the play will be balanced by floating corpses. Every white cloud in the blue sky will remind Baal of the white corpse in the river. The struggle will be everywhere an epic contest, and man will only be able to sing to himself as Baal sings to himself, as he dances: "Tanz mit dem Wind, armer Leichnam, schlaf mit der Wolke, verkommener Gott!" (p. 51).

Man will be depicted not as misunderstood, but as not understanding—far closer to the biblical mentality of the Prophets and of the Wisdom literature. The beggar of the thirteenth scene, *Hölzerne braune Diele*, tells the story of man in a way that reflects both Brecht's origin in the Black Forest and an attitude of mind on the question of the meaning of human existence far closer to Ecclesiastes than to *Der Einsame*:

> Ich kannte einen Mann, der meinte auch, er sei gesund. Meinte es. Er stammte aus einem Wald und kam einmal wieder dort hin, denn er mußte sich etwas überlegen. Den Wald fand er sehr fremd und nicht mehr verwandt. Viele Tage ging er, ganz hinauf in die Wildnis, denn er wollte sehen, wie weit er abhängig war und wieviel noch in ihm war, daß er's aushielte. Aber es war nicht mehr viel. *Trinkt.*
> . . .
> Ja, der Wind. An einem Abend, um die Dämmerung, als er nicht mehr so allein war, ging er durch die große Stille zwischen die Bäume und stellte sich unter einen von ihnen, der sehr groß war. *Trinkt.*
> . . .
> . . . Er lehnte sich an ihn, ganz nah, fühlte das Leben in ihm, oder meinte es und sagte: Du bist höher als ich und stehst fest und du kennst die Erde bis tief hinunter und sie hält dich. Ich kann laufen und mich besser bewegen, aber ich stehe nicht fest und kann nicht in die Tiefe und nichts hält mich. Auch ist mir die große Ruhe über den stillen Wipfeln im unendlichen Himmel unbekannt. *Trinkt.*
> Gougou: Was sagte der Baum?
> Der Bettler: Ja, Der Wind ging. Durch den Baum lief ein Zittern, der Mann fühlte es. Da warf er sich zu Boden, umschlang die wilden und harten Wurzeln und weinte bitterlich. . . . (pp. 47–48)

This prose-poem is, I believe, something of very great beauty, and of spiritual depth. "To lean upon the tree" is almost made significant and repeated in the manner of a Homeric epithet in *Baal* and yet the quality of the walking through the stillness between the trees reminds one of the walking in the garden in the cool of the evening in Genesis. Even Goethe's evening quiet is included, though disclaimed. The dominant image is the rustling of the tree by the moving nothingness, the wind. The man ends up both embracing the roots of the tree of life and, with Peter, crying bitterly. The tree of life will live long, its roots are hard and deep, it is an old bio-religious relation of the man or his race before it, but the space between the trees, with the cold moving wind, is older yet, and will be there a long time after the old tree shall have fallen.

Thus Brecht has used the Baal myth from the Bible and "the Wind" from the prophets and Wisdom writers who wrote against the cult or who were too skeptical to take it seriously. I think in recognizing this fact we also have answered the problem of the controversial last Scene 22, *Frühe im Wald*. While many editions do not include it, and dramatically it is quite difficult to get an audience to recover for it from the powerful effect of watching Baal crawl to the door at the end of the usually final Scene 21, *Bretterhütte im Wald*, still, Brecht did want it included,[16] and it does accord well with the biblical Baal myth. It incorporates the possibility of cyclic return even in the midst of schnaps and vulgarity. It provides the Brechtian device of the run-on scene (used in *Mahagonny* and *Mutter Courage*) which follows the climactic ending scene, allowing final comment on the climax. In both *Mahagonny* and *Mutter Courage* the additional scene signifies the tragic continuance of things, indifferently, after the death of the hero. The world goes on, hardly noticing an individual death. In *Baal*, however, there are some nuances. The lumberjacks are indeed coldly indifferent to the death of Baal, but the third lumberjack is able to tell the audience Baal's last words, words that change the "Hm," which leaves the ultimate resolution to the audience, to "Regen," which leaves it to the cosmos, perhaps, and to myth: "Dritter: Ich frage ihn, wie er schon röchelt in der Gurgel hinten: An was denkst du? Ich will immer wissen, was man da denkt. Da sagte er: Ich horche noch auf den Regen. Mir lief eine Gänsehaut über den Buckel. Ich horche noch auf den Regen, sagte er" (p. 67).

The following outline commentary will enable the reader to see some of the major Brechtian biblical allusions in *Baal* in proper sequence. This is important prior to going on to consider his use of the Passion and Death accounts.

Table 2

Baal	*The Bible*
Der Choral vom großen Baal	in antipsalmic style, parody of a Christian hymn.
der Himmel, nackt	ironic application to the heavens of the Wisdom-tradition evaluation of man (esp. in Eccl 5:15): Wie er nackend ist von seiner Mutter

Table 2 (*continued*)

	Leibe kommen, so fährt er wieder hin, wie er kommen ist (und nimmt nichts mit sich von seiner Arbeit in seiner Hand, wenn er hinfähret). (Also in Job 1:21, Ps 49:18; Wis 7:6; 1 Tim 6:7.)
Sterne, düster	reversal of wisdom commonplace of the stars as speaking of The One Beyond and His glory, e.g., Ps 8:4: "Denn ich werde sehen die Himmel, deiner Finger Werk, den Mond und die Sterne, die du bereitest. Was ist der Mensch, daß du sein gedenkest . . ." or Job 38:31–33 on the Pleiades and Orion as God's doing.
In der Sünder schamvollem Gewimmel; in dem Jammertal	Popular preaching tradition.
Sc. 2: *Baals Dachkammer* (*Sternennacht. Sie sehen Himmel*) die Erde eine Kugel	astronomical orientation: cold cosmos, enemy of life's egocentricity and warmth; reinforcement through science of ironic use of Ps 8 and Eccl 5:15.
ein neuer Kosmos	ironic use of biblical commonplace of the new cosmos, the new heavens and the new earth, cf. Rev 21:1, inserted delightfully into the context of a biologizing reflection on pregnancy and birth.
Wenn du die jungfräulichen Hüften umschlingst, wirst du in der Angst und Seligkeit der Kreatur zum Gott. (Baal to Johannes)	Gen 3, the temptation of the serpent: *Eritis sicut Deus*, translated into sexual "theology."

Table 2 *(continued)*

Sc. 3: *Branntweinschenke* daß du ein Mensch nur bist, der nichts behalten darf.	vulgarization of Eccl 5:15, and popular preaching tradition association with it.
Gott hat einen vergessen	reversal of biblical tradition that God does not forget, e.g., Gen 8:1— Da gedachte Gott an Noah (will be used in next scene); and Is 49:14–15 —Zion aber spricht: "Der Herr hat mich verlassen, der Herr hat mein vergessen." Kann ach ein Weib ihres Kindleins vergessen . . .? Und ob sie desselbigen vergäße, so will ich doch dein nicht vergessen.
Sc. 4: *Baals Dachkammer* Morgengrauen auf dem Berg Ararat.	Noah's landing point after the Flood. Gen 8:4 (Johanna's drowning) also sobriety after drinking.
die ägyptische Finsternis	the darkness prior to the Exodus.
Der weiße Schnaps ist mein Stecken und Stab.	Brechtification of Ps 23:4—Derr Herr ist mein Hirte . . . dein Stecken und Stab trösten mich.
Es ist der April. Es wird dunkel, und du riechst mich. So ist es bei den Tieren. (Baal to Sophie)	Baal myth. Cf. Is and Hosea 13.
Wir legen uns unter die Pflanzen. . . . Die Weiden am Fluß tropfnaß, vom Regen struppig. Du mußt bleiche Schenkel haben.	Baal worship. Cf. Is 57 and Hosea 13: Rain, vegetation, sex "under every green tree."
Sc. 5: *Gekalkte Häuser mit braunen Baumstämmen*	*Fronleichnam* (Corpus Christi) reinterpreted as the crucifixion of life (Baumkadaver and Frauenleiber identified by Baal) by Christianity.
Sc. 6: *Mainacht unter Bäumen* Regen . . . Das Gras muß noch	Baal myth. Baal as Rain-god,

Table 2 *(continued)*

naß sein . . . Das junge Laub trieft von Nässe, aber hier in den Wurzeln ist es trocken. Warum kann man nicht mit den Pflanzen schlafen?	worship of Baal under the trees of intercourse.
Mai, jetzt drei Wochen	Baal myth, cf. April above, November below.
Sc. 7: *Nachtcafé "Zur Wolke in der Nacht"* Blaue Pflaumen fraß das Kind Und den sanften weißen Leib Ließ es still dem Zeitvertreib.	"plums" and sexual activity explains sexual symbol used in following scenes: Pflaumenbäume.
Sc. 8: *Grüne Felder, blaue Pflaumenbäume*	"figtrees" of Baal myth. Hosea 2:10 ff.
Sc. 9: *Dorfschenke,* die Stiere der Pfarrer (as also die Hausfrau of Sc. 2)	animal of the Baal cult, used as a joke the biblical "good man" for Brecht?
Sc. 10: *Bäume am Abend* Es ist eine Eiche gewesen. Er war nicht gleich tot, sondern litt noch.	trees, life symbol of Baal cult. Image, conflating man and tree in death; lying in the grass, perhaps suggested by subsequent discussion. Eccl 11:3–4—und wenn der Baum fällt, er falle gegen Mittag oder Mitternacht, auf welchen Ort er fällt, da wird er liegen—also uses the same image of the fallen tree to express the absoluteness of death and may possibly have suggested this image of the oak.
Das Wetter . . . grün mit etwas Regen.	Baal, rain-god, weather-god.
Im Gras ein Leichnam	Mot.
Der Himmel ist schwarz	astronomy, not Ps 8, on the heavens.
Holzfäller, an Bäume gelehnt	Mot and Baal.

Table 2 *(continued)*

Könnt ihr nicht ein wenig an den armen Teddy denken?	Suggests Christ's question in Agony in the Garden: Könntet ihr nicht eine Stunde mit mir wachen? Mt 26:40 (again in Sc. 21 at Baal's death).
Er stinkt immer noch nicht.	possibly verbal allusion to Lazarus's grave scene where Martha says: Herr, er stinkt schon, denn er ist vier Tage gelegen. Jn 11:39.
(Baal to Teddy's corpse) . . . deine Seele war eine verflucht noble Persönlichkeit, die Wohnung war schadhaft, und die Ratten verlassen das sinkende Schiff . . .	ironic rephrasing of Christ's comment on the sleeping disciples (again from the Agony in the Garden as immediately above!) Mt 26:41— Der Geist ist willig, aber das Fleisch ist schwach.
Gott sei seiner besoffenen Seele gnädig!	"adapted" from liturgical prayers for the dead.
Er ist der hart-gesottenste Sünder, der zwischen Gottes Händen herumläuft.	adaptation of popular preaching tradition.
Seht euch den Himmel an zwischen den Bäumen, der jetzt dunkel wird. Ist das nichts? Dann habt ihr keine Religion im Leibe!	common New Testament teaching formula, e.g., Mt 6:26—Sehet (euch) die Vögel unter dem Himmel an, usw. Here reversed to assert the presence of death and nothing, Mot and the void.
Sc. 11: *Eine Hütte* Man hört regnen. (Baal to Ekart)— Du bist ein böser Mensch, gerade wie ich, ein Teufel.	Baal, Rain-god. Baal-zebub. Allusion to Baal being regarded as the devil in popular tradition.
Sc. 12: *Ebene. Himmel.* homo- & hetero-sexuality Heut ist Johannis (Baal to Ekart) —Komm, ich erzähle dir von den Tieren.	Baal cult. Midsummer. Baal, god of annual life cycle, Baal cult.

Table 2 *(continued)*

Sc. 13: *Hölzerne braune Diele*
(Nacht. Wind.)

The Beggar's story

parabolic style with biblical
expressions such as "er warf sich zu
Boden."

Der Wind ging. Da warf er sich zu
Boden, umschlang die wilden und
harten Wurzeln und weinte
bitterlich.

Passion and Death account: Peter
after the cock crew. Mt 26:75—Und
er ging hinaus und weinte bitterlich.
Here used of man's reaction to the
death even of the old and hardy in
life, the ancient tree, when the wind
blows.

Tanz mit dem Wind, armer
Leichnam, schlaf mit der Wolke,
verkommener Gott!

Baal and Mot.

Sc. 15: *Landstraße. Weiden.*
(Wind. Nacht.)

Und der Abend ward abends
                    dunkel wie Rauch
Und hielt nachts mit den Sternen
                    das Licht in Schwebe
Aber früh ward er hell, daß es auch
Noch für sie Morgen und Abend
                    gebe.
Als ihr bleicher Leib im Wasser
                    verfaulet war
Geschah es, sehr langsam, daß
          Gott sie allmählich vergaß:
Erst ihr Gesicht, dann die Hände
          und ganz zuletzt erst ihr Haar.
Dann ward sie Aas in Flüssen mit
                    vielem Aas.

anti-Genesis antiphon: Da ward
aus Abend und Morgen der erste
Tag. Cf. Gen 1: 4–5—Da schied
Gott das Licht von der Finsternis,
und nannte das Licht Tag und die
Finsternis Nacht. Da ward aus
Abend und Morgen der erste Tag.
(Cf. Brecht's *Lobet die Finsternis*
in the *Hauspostille*.) Remembering-
forgetting, biblical terms for the
Divine Awareness. Here used to
imply there is a lack thereof in the
case of the dying. Cf. "Mein Gott,
Mein Gott, warum hast du mich
verlassen" in *Die Bibel*.

Ich sehe die Welt im milden Licht:
sie ist das Exkrement Gottes.

vulgarization of the orifice from
which the world is pictured as
coming from God. Biblical tradition
is the mouth: God *said*, Let there be,
etc., In the beginning was the *Word*
and through him has been made all
that has been made. (Gen 1 and Jn 1)

Table 2 *(continued)*

Sc. 17: *Ahorn im Wind*	Is. 57:13.
. . .	
Und sie sahn ihn sich am Baume halten Und sie hörten, wie er ihnen schrie. Und es graute ihnen so wie nie Daß sie zitternd ihre Fäuste ballten: Denn er war ein Mann wie sie.	Biblical verse style; Crucifixion?
. . .	
Und sie sahn noch nach dem Baume hin Unter den sie eingegraben ihn Dem das Sterben allzu bitter schien: Der Baum war oben voll Licht. Und sie bekreuzten ihr junges Gesicht Und sie ritten schnell in die Prärien.	After cruelty, religiosity— Resurrection through the tree?
Sc. 18: *Branntweinschenke* Ihr Mörder, denen viel Leides geschah!/Warum seid ihr nicht im Schoß eurer Mütter geblieben?	Job's curse on the day he was born: Warum bin ich nicht gestorben von Mutterleib an? Warum hat man mich auf den Schoß gesetzet? (Job 3:11–12)
Watzmann: Es werde Licht. Baal: Das blendet.	Gen. 1:3.
Sc. 19: *10° Ö. L. von Greenwich*	Baal myth; cold and death of winter are identified.
Sc. 20: *Landstraße. Regen. Wind.*	Baal. Mot.
Allerseelenwind!	November, Baal myth. Christian feast of the Dead (All Souls). Baal killed by Mot. Death of Baal-Tammuz and ritual weeping found in Ex 8: 13–14.

Table 2 *(continued)*

Tot also? Armes Tierchen!	Similar to Eccl 3:19—Denn es gehet dem Menschen, wie dem Vieh; wie dies stirbt, so stirbt er auch; und haben alle einerlei Odem; und der Mensch hat nichts mehr, denn das Vieh; denn es ist alles eitel. (Cf. frequent use of animals as men and men as animals in Baal to connote mortality.)
Sc. 21: *Bretterhütte im Wald* Habe keine Angst: Die Welt rollt weiter, kugelrund, morgen früh pfeift der Wind.	possibly Eccl 1:2–6, as above.
Die Männer (stehen auf): Jetzt hat der Regen aufgehört. Es ist Zeit.	Baal myth and Passion and Death of Christ. Death of Baal (rain ceased), beginning of Passion suggested from Mt 26:18—Meine Zeit ist hie—but put into the more familiar biblical form without problem of blasphemy.
Könnt ihr nicht noch etwas dableiben? . . . Wenn ihr noch dreißig Minuten bliebet.	Mt 26:40, Agony in Garden— Könntet ihr denn nicht eine Stunde mit mir wachen? (Christ's reproach to the indifference of the sleeping disciples.)
Anderer Mann: . . . Da hast du was zum Andenken! (Spuckt ihm ins Gesicht). (This has followed general mockery *in großem Gelächter*)	Passion and Death: Mt 26: 67—Da spien sie ihm ins Gesicht.
Wisch den Speichel weg! Wo? Auf der Stirn.	Veronica legend.
Kruzifix. Leichname!	The Cross. Cf. Sc. 5: *Fronleichnam*. Brecht frequently uses "accidental" blasphemies of this type in a way suggestive of their original meaning;

Table 2 *(continued)*

	cf. the Bäuerin in *Mutter Courage* who shouts "Jesus" when she hears Kattrin's first drumbeats.
Lieber Baal! (In the 1918 version this was: Lieber Gott!)[17]	prayer or exclamation.
Sc. 22: *Frühe im Wald* Holzfäller: Ich frage ihn, wie er schon röchelt . . . ich horche noch auf den Regen, sagte er.	Baal myth. Spring rain, rebirth.

From the above outline commentary it can be seen quite clearly, I believe, that the Baal myth and the Baal cult from the Old Testament and possibly the handbook, are the backbone for the structure of the entire play. I think it is also clear that, in addition to the passages from Isaiah and Hosea used for *Baal*, Brecht seems to favor two other Old Testament sources in *Baal*: Genesis and Ecclesiastes.[18]

Genesis is used to reinforce the early scenes of sexual temptation by jokingly serious, occasional uses of commonplaces from the scene in the Garden of Eden. A paraphrase of the serpent's *eritis sicut Deus* is said by Baal to Johannes, as well as a vulgarized paraphrase of *Staub soll er fressen*. Brecht's alienation of these phrases is used not simply to poke fun at the old meanings, but also to open them up to a new and more sexual interpretation (which in the mouth of Baal is most fitting), and to add a more sinister level to what otherwise might become just a comic sex scene in the play.

Genesis, and its God, is attacked bitterly in the later scenes where its old familiar clichés are made to stand confronted with death in all its biophysical reality. As the cadaver degenerates in the water, Brecht is incapable of reacting scientifically or of expressing his reaction in scientific terms. He is simply unable to take any less than an outraged religious viewpoint. For this he needs Genesis, to express his almost metaphysical disappointment and outrage: "morning and evening came, another day," as the body falls apart. The text is removed from its usual biblical place, where it marks the progress of God creating life, and put into the context of death, where it poignantly exposes the sovereign indifference of the God of Genesis to the progress of death. This curious mixture of nonacceptance and respect with which Brecht seems to view Genesis's treatment of darkness and death is startlingly revealed again near the end of the play

(Scene 18) where Watzmann, lighting a lamp, says jokingly, "Es werde Licht!" and Baal answers, "Das blendet." This frequent use of Genesis, whether estranged or not, keeps the audience down on that primeval level where life, death, the tree in the Garden, and the darkness are still tremendous and powerful realities. These primitive forces cause more the anguish of questioning the reality of God in the universe rather than the place of poets in society—even in the controlled world of Augsburg, the café, and the fields.

The book of Ecclesiastes, unlike Genesis, has a single dominating characteristic that must have made it most amenable to the author of Baal: the book is totally preoccupied with the annihilating reality of death. "Vanity of vanities, all is emptiness and a chasing after the wind" (Eccl 1:1–9). Like almost all the authors of the Old Testament, Ecclesiastes has no real belief in a *Jenseits* for men, and thus, like Brecht, considers men to be no better off than animals (3:16–21), who are born and die naked (5:15–19), and who tragically seek after things that are foolish to obtain since they can't be held (Ch. 1–4). He counsels therefore, "Eat drink and be merry. . . ." (3:12–13), as does Baal, and advises a more or less amoral treasuring of life while it lasts, "better a live dog than a dead lion" (9:3–10), for men are cruel to each other (4:1–3 & 5:7–9), and all is for nothing anyway: "One generation comes, another goes, while the sun rises and the sun sets, and the wind blows. . . ." (1:4–6). "And if a tree fall to the south or to the north, in whatsoever place the tree falls, there shall it be" (11:3–4).

Aside from the few specific instances of citation indicated in the outline commentary, one cannot be certain to what extent Brecht was influenced by the imagery of Ecclesiastes, but it is surprisingly similar to his own in *Baal*. Perhaps it is another case of his famous (or infamous) nondisclosure of sources! However this may be, it is certain that he uses wind with the same double meaning of cosmic indifference to the death of men, as well as the nothingness of the void and vanity and death—which is the same symbolic value it has in Ecclesiastes and in Isaiah *when Isaiah is speaking against the Baal cult*. Brecht does not use this image in an alienated way, as he frequently does with texts of Genesis, but uses it with its original meaning in the Bible—and he reinforces it further with astronomy and biology. He thus uses it in a way sympathetic to its original use and context, but he accentuates the cruelty of its truth, the coldness of the wind's indifference, and by this means gains sympathy for the outcast Baal.

Brecht's use of the New Testament, here mainly from Matthew's Passion, is even more "sympathetic." The Passion and Death account is used only in the two death scenes—that of Teddy (Scene 10), and the climactic scene of the death of Baal (Scene 21). By restricting its use this way, Brecht deliberately focuses far more emotion on these two scenes than on any other. This is a tendency that will be manifest again in *Mahagonny*, and even more impressively in *Mutter Courage*.

Scene 10, *Bäume am Abend*, is a scene of death—indicated not only by the *am Abend*, in this context, but also by the presence of a corpse in the grass. *Holzfäller* indicates the paradox of which Brecht is so fond, both here and in *Mutter Courage*, of how living things sustain their life by death and taking life, of how *Bäume* are nourished by the *Aas* at their roots, of how lumberjacks "lean on" trees.

In this scene a further death, the coldness of people to people, is expressed and reproved through the suggestion of the biblical reproof of Christ to his disciples' coldness to his Agony, "Könnt ihr nicht ein wenig an den armen Teddy denken?" Even more than this indifference, the indifference of Heaven (or the heavens) is expressed and attacked by the astronomically indisputable statement that the lumberjacks reject as absurd—"Der Himmel ist schwarz." The length of time that the corpse is dead is stated philosophically, "Er war" and reinforced with concrete biblical verbal allusion: "er stinkt immer noch nicht." Teddy's leg is lifted up to attack the Christian body/soul distinction (as already done in *Die Bibel*) and we hear Brecht's Baalic persiflage—"the spirit is willing but the flesh is weak"—so paraphrased that we are effectively repelled both by the facileness with which Christians forfeit the body, and by the ease with which the body breaks down! It is also humorous, blackly humorous, to hear the dark Brecht hermeneutic of Mt. 26:41, "Die Wohnung war schadhaft, und die Ratten verlassen das sinkende Schiff."

The scene ends with a question suggesting the nature of the divine entity as revealed by the sight of this corpse in the grass, which stinketh, "Ist das nichts?"—a question which, like the "Sterne . . . Hm." of the ending, leaves the ultimate religious question squarely in the hands of the audience.

In the climax, Scene 21, *Bretterhütte im Wald*, scripture is used in the context of the death of the god who is very much a man, Baal. Theologically it might border on the absurd to have the dying Baal made into a suffering Christ, but not in human terms. Brecht uses the Passion and Death here to subject all things to death, including the Christ and Baal of the Bible, as well as to gain sympathy for human weakness, in this case the ultimate human weakness, dying. Baal's struggle to stay alive begins with the beautiful combination of the biblical "Es ist Zeit," from Christ's beginning Passion, with the stopping of the rains in the Baal myth. Both the pagan and the Christian scriptures, *David cum Sybilla*, announce that the end has come. In this simple phrase and stage direction the whole play is brought together for its ending.

The agony of the world's indifference has already been told to Baal in language reminiscent of Ecclesiastes 1:2–6, by the first *Mann* in Scene 21: "Habe keine Angst: die Welt rollt weiter, kugelrund, morgen früh pfeift der Wind." The indifference of humankind is made all the more cold through the use, this time much more explicitly than in the case of Teddy's death, of Christ's own statement of loneliness to the disciples in the Garden: "Könnt ihr nicht noch etwas dableiben? . . . Wenn ihr noch dreißig Minuten bliebet." Baal even shortens Christ's request for *eine Stunde* to an even more considerate half-hour! After the mocking and spitting, Baal dies alone, crawling out of the door into the night. The power of the scene lies in the primeval tenacity with which Baal clings to life by any means possible—brilliantly put together in his last speech. Calling out in vain even to himself (in the 1918 version he was openly calling out to God), Baal crawls out of the November door with, as it were, the spit of Christ's mockers upon him.

Perhaps the key to *Baal*'s "theology" lies in this striving for the door.[19] Even in death Baal is looking for life, light and the door. He has pleaded for companionship, sex, music; he has called out to his mother, to numbers, and to himself. He has asked Ekart to come and to go away. In vivid poetry, Brecht has dismissed poetry as an ultimate concern and reasserted the value of life by pointing to its sovereign enemy: the wind. He has pointed out for our time, in scientific and antiscientific, poetic and antipoetic, religious and antireligious language that we are, as the ancients said, at base not scientists, not poets, nor moral beings, but mortals. Perhaps mortal gods: "And it may rain again in the spring."

A theologian's summary of the Baal cult provides an interesting parallel for a final summary of *Baal*.

Baalism was a danger to Israelite belief not merely because of its obscenities but also because it was nature worship which reduced YHWH to the level of a personified natural force and made religion no more than a means of securing the good of nature. Ultimately the cult was a denial of any moral values or of any transcendental reality.[20]

IV

Mahagonny: No New Jerusalem

Between *Baal* and *Aufstieg und Fall der Stadt Mahagonny* there lie another ten years. Brecht is now thirty and in Berlin. He returns again to using the image of the city and once more it is the apocalyptic city of *Die Bibel*, threatened this time not by external enemies, but by the deep fears and mistrust within it. Mahagonny is the ultimate Miami, the "American" pleasure city where anything goes—as long as you can pay for it.

In the intervening ten years between *Baal* and *Mahagonny* Brecht had become thoroughly acquainted with the Marxist critique of economic capitalism, and this critique was as important to *Mahagonny* as biology was to *Baal*. The great enemy of man, this time, is not so much his ultimate weakness, mortality, but rather socio-economic weakness, especially the ultimate "mortal sin," not having any money. Responsibility for a society that has evolved such a degrading way of estimating the goodness or badness, the worth, of the individual man is laid squarely at the feet of Leokadja Begbick—the middle-class business instinct—and of "Dreieinigkeitsmoses"—the Judaeo-Christian tradition.

Brecht's social concern does not permit him a total escape, however, from his metaphysical fear that death might render all attempts at reform and revolution pointless. At the end of the play death will once more be the only absolute present. Death's only possible serious opponent, God, shows up in *Mahagonny* only *mitten im Whisky*. *Mahagonny* has much less of the prankish youthful air of *Baal*, and after a prolonged sally (accompanied by Weill's music) into the realms of the social, the moral, and the theological, the play returns again at the end, far more somberly than in *Baal*, to the reason for the awful futility of any effort of any kind:

> Können einem toten Mann nicht helfen.
> Können uns und euch und niemand helfen. (GW, II, 564)

The weakness of not being able to help is a note sounded again and again in Brecht from *Die Bibel* to *Mutter Courage*. At best, man can keep going despite almost all that his vices bring upon him and de-

spite almost all his enemies—except one. We will return to discuss
the possible underlying Brechtian "theology" that leads to this view
of man after we have demonstrated his use of the Bible in the play.

In May 1927, Charles Lindbergh made the first solo flight across the
Atlantic. This tremendous accomplishment of an individual, a tri-
umphing over the wind and the water, provided the writer of *Baal*
with the inspiration to write *Der Flug der Lindberghs* in the period
1928–29, the same period in which he wrote *Mahagonny*. In order to
understand the role of "God" in *Mahagonny* it is useful to examine
the more explicit role of God in *Der Ozeanflug*.[1] Here a man (or rather
a group of men, because Brecht follows the Marxist notion of considering the pilot and the factory workers one, and thus uses the
plural) has triumphed—even if only temporarily—over Brecht's symbols for the meaningless abyss and death: the water and the wind. All
that without any help from God! As long as Brecht can keep his eyes
off his corpses in the water, he can glory in the escape of the Lindberghs from the finite conditions of human existence. They have put
their heads into the lion's mouth and have come out unharmed. In
the chapter marked *Ideologie* (GW, II, 575) he fairly rhapsodizes on the
triumph of weak man over wind and water:

> Die Dampfschiffe sind gegen die Segler gefahren
> Welche die Ruderboote hinter sich zurückließen.
> Ich
> Fliege gegen die Dampfschiffe
> Im Kampf gegen das Primitive.
> Mein Flugzeug, schwach und zittrig
> Meine Apparate voller Mangel
> Sind besser als die bisherigen, aber
> Indem ich fliege
> Kämpfe ich gegen mein Flugzeug und
> Gegen das Primitive. (GW, II, 575–76)

The victory of the weak, pyrrhic or not, is something that Brecht
seems to find stirring, whenever it may happen. He is not afraid to
admit the weaknesses of the aircraft or technology, he is not afraid to
admit that in the beginning the fliers just barely decided to keep
going at the time when the fog rose up against them.

> Wenn keine Aussicht da ist
> Kämpfe ich nicht weiter.
> Entweder mit dem Schild oder auf dem Schild
> Mache ich nicht mit.

Aber jetzt
Kehre ich noch nicht um. (GW, II, 571)

More importantly, the exaltation of flying over the void and of just barely missing the crests of the waters brings forth an even more strongly antitheological statement from the flier(s):

Was immer ich bin und welche Dummheiten ich glaube
Wenn ich fliege, bin ich
Ein wirklicher Atheist. (GW, II, 576)

In this paradoxical statement we have praise for the freeing of oneself from the God-idea—even if this freedom occurs only when one is engaged in fighting the primeval and primitive elements—and an admission of stupidities that are believed when one is not "flying." Though in most Brecht plays there is deep sadness whenever the note of "mein Gott, mein Gott, warum hast du mich verlassen" is struck, here there is exultation in attaining, even if only for a transient period, the state of a–theism. Just as in *Baal* it was promised that one would become like God in sex, here it it promised in flying, "Wenn ich fliege, bin ich. . . ." Preoccupation with doing, with technology, with the motor and machinery, will clear the ultimate questions from our minds, will drive the specter of God from our skies and will replace it with airplanes.

Brecht's brief antitheology in this play treats the origin of God in the popular Marxist materialist way, not in relation to the problem of the actual existence versus the possible nonexistence of the entire world (Creation), nor in relation to the problem of the life versus death of the individual human being, but rather as a construct of the imagination of the deprived, pretechnological era. This uncomplicated point of view Brecht expounds well here, and even seems to maintain it in "stählerner Einfalt." As a result there is less biblicizing in *Der Ozeanflug* than in any of the pieces by Brecht that we are considering. His legitimate rejoicing in Lindbergh's feat—"Tausend Jahre fiel alles von oben nach unten/Ausgenommen der Vogel"— gave him a moment of simple atheism, a moment in which he could let "flying" distract him from dying down below on the earth, and in which he could let a "motor" give him the meaning for living and drown out some of the dark concerns of his own pretechnological poetic imagination.

Zehntausend Jahre lang entstand
Wo die Wasser dunkel wurden am Himmel
Zwischen Licht und Dämmerung unhinderbar

Gott. Und ebenso
Über den Gebirgen, woher das Eis kam
Sichteten die Unwissenden
Unbelehrbar Gott, und ebenso
In den Wüsten kam er im Sandsturm, und
In den Städten wurde er erzeugt von der Unordnung
Der Menschenklassen, weil es zweierlei Menschen gibt
Ausbeutung und Unkenntnis, aber
Die Revolution liquidiert ihn. Aber
Baut Straßen durch die Gebirge, dann verschwindet er
Flüsse vertreiben ihn aus der Wüste. Das Licht
Zeigt Leere und
Verscheucht ihn sofort.

Darum beteiligt euch
An der Bekämpfung des Primitiven
An der Liquidierung des Jenseits und
Der Verscheuchung jedweden Gottes, wo
Immer er auftaucht.

Unter den schärferen Mikroskopen
Fällt er.
Es vertreiben ihn
Die verbesserten Apparate aus der Luft.
Die Reinigung der Städte
Die Vernichtung des Elends
Machen ihn verschwinden und
Jagen ihn zurück in das erste Jahrtausend.
(GW, II, 576–77)

Brecht seems to have realized though, both at this time and later in
Galilei, that the God who is driven out by technology, driven out of
the mountains (from which the ice came) by roadways, is not the God
about whom he is really worried, the God in whose existence he
really would like to believe or disbelieve. The "God" whom theo-
logians call "the god of the interstices," that is, the God who is used
as the explanation for all the gaps in our knowledge of the universe
and who popularly pops up in orthodox clothing as an excuse for our
not laboring further to do the difficult or to discover the unknown ("if
God wanted men to fly, he would have given them wings," etc.) is a
god whom the poet and the medical student Brecht allows himself a
moment to cast out and "shoo off." The real God, however, about
whose existence or nonexistence Brecht always seems to be agoniz-
ing, is the God of the dying weak—of the stolid grandfather praying

helplessly as the city burns, of Baal alone and abandoned, crawling, dragging himself to the door to see the stars, of those killed by the *Luftwaffe* Lindbergh praised, of dumb Kattrin shot on top of the roof, and even in this same year of 1928, of Paul Ackermann, executed for having no money, while quoting Scripture and asking for a glass of water. It is possible for Brecht, at one and the same time, to write of Lindbergh's flight and of Paul Ackermann's death, since he does not believe in the god of the interstices, but seems to wonder about whether there is a God to receive those who are meaninglessly killed by this world.

Mahagonny begins where *Baal* left off—with the future of the hard-working lumberjacks, the *Holzfäller*. After they have earned their money in the north, chopping down trees, what reward is there for them? What can one do with the money that one earns by the sweat of one's brow? What in the West would be the most enjoyable thing they could do with it?

A place is founded for them to go to, a net is woven to trap and exploit their human weaknesses and to make money off their need for enjoyment: the city. The founding fathers of this trap are: sex (the girls), business instinct (the widow Begbick and Willy), and Judaeo-Christians (Trinity-Moses). As one might anticipate from that com-bination, the Bible is used far more bitterly in this play than in any other. The character *Dreieinigkeitsmoses* is present throughout the play as a caricature of Western religion, leading the procession, carrying out the will of widow Begbick, and executing consequences on any-one who runs afoul of her. Through Trinity-Moses's constant pres-ence Brecht lays partial blame for the founding and continuation of the evils of the "trap," the capitalistic, American/German business city, upon the active collaboration of the Judaeo-Christians.

Despite the fact that the scene is cast in the most Western of coun-tries, and in a geography that (according to the songs) fluctuates between the palm trees of Florida and the warm moonlit nights of rural Alabama (with California's West-coast gold not too far away), Brecht sees to it that the play begins in a desert, and with a Moses leading us ever onward through the desert, saying, "Aber wir müs-sen weiter" (GW, II, 501). This mock Exodus is even provided with the traditional protest of the faint-hearted, "Also müssen wir um-kehren," which is, however, thwarted not by the leadership of Trinity-Moses, nor even by a pursuing army of Egyptian regulars, but rather by the pursuing police. The "Exodus" here has renounced any pos-sible spiritual meaning of the human journey and has been com-pletely demythologized so as to be made entirely materialistic, and profitable, here on earth. The widow Begbick communicates this new insight to us when she pokes her head out of the truck and comments on the impossibility of going up to the far away gold coast: "Es ist mir eingefallen: wenn wir nicht hinaufkommen können, werden wir hier unten bleiben" (GW, II, 502). Since they cannot get to the gold coast themselves, they will stay here and get gold from people, and "weil alles so schlecht ist" (GW, II, 503), what else should they do anyway? In any case, "Ihr bekommt leichter das Gold von Männern als von Flüssen" (GW, II, 502).

Not only is there no high purpose whatsoever to this Exodus, but now Moses, the Widow and the Bookkeeper form the three-cornered basis of a "new Creation," a "new Jerusalem" for the money culture of the modern world. In words that are again taken from the Creation and Naming accounts of Genesis, distorted somewhat in the name of an "improved" Garden of Paradise, Brecht describes the origin of the city in biblical cadences:

> Darum laßt uns hier eine Stadt gründen
> Und sie nennen Mahagonny
> Das heißt: Netzestadt!
> Sie soll sein wie ein Netz
> Das für die eßbaren Vögel gestellt wird.
> Überall gibt es Mühe und Arbeit
> Aber hier gibt es Spaß.
> . . .
> Gin und Whisky
> Mädchen und Knaben.
> Und eine Woche ist hier: sieben Tage ohne Arbeit.
> (GW, II, 502)

In this capitalists' paradise, there is the ultimate in bliss offered to the working class, not just a Sabbath rest every weekend, but seven days a week without work! Of course, this is only as long as one has the money from the previous sweat of one's brow to be able to pay for it. Brecht goes so far as to use the traditional biblical image in the passage for the innocent being trapped: the birds in the fowler's snare. Once again Ecclesiastes seems to have made an impression on Brecht: "For man does not know his time; like fish that are caught in an evil net, or like birds caught in a snare, so are the sons of men snared in an evil time as it falls upon them suddenly." (Eccl 9:12)[2]

Smoothed into the general biblical speech of Begbick's first song on the founding of the city with a name like a tree (which, in the irony of the life cycle, is what *Holzfäller* fell) and on the pleasures it will offer, are certain foreboding statements that let us know that Brecht with the skull on the table and Baal on the wall is not too far away from Brecht the communist:

> Und die großen Taifune kommen nicht bis hierher.
> Aber die Männer ohne Zank
> Erwarten rauchend das Heraufkommen des Abends.
> (GW, II, 502–503)

Willy and Trinity-Moses confirm an even darker, less socially-integrated reason for the founding of the city than the one old Begbick gave. The city has been founded only "weil alles so schlecht ist, weil keine Ruhe herrscht und keine Eintracht" (GW, II, 503). They then go even a level deeper than the social and economic disorder of the late twenties and the Depression, the negative side of the in-flight atheism of the new technological Lindbergh culture:

> Und weil es nichts gibt
> Woran man sich halten kann. (GW, II, 503)

The underlying opportunistic nihilism of the cities is made evident not only by this statement, but it is made even more religiously tragic by having it be said by *Dreieinigkeitsmoses* himself.

The one bird who will try to escape from the fowler's net will be Paul Ackermann/Jimmy Mahonney. Human weakness, however, will keep him trapped. Having the Brechtian fatal flaw of caring, being concerned about his friend Alaskawolf Joe, he bets all he has on Joe in his boxing match with Trinity-Moses and loses it when Joe is knocked out. Paul/Jimmy will then be executed after the *Spiel von Gott in Mahagonny* for having committed the one enormity still possible in amoral Net City: having no money.

Brecht uses the Bible throughout the play in the same double pattern we have seen before: his attacks on capitalism will be made by exposing capitalism as a form of idolatry, an antihuman worship of money. This he does by revealing the "sacred origins" of the city and by "blessing" the founding of the city and its continuance with quotations from Genesis, the Wisdom literature and Psalms, and by generally putting biblical language into the mouths of the undesirables who run the city—whether from Old Testament or New Testament commonplace formulae. However, since the hero dies out of human involvement and human compassion, Brecht again surrounds him with an aura of the events of the Passion and Death. Peter's denial is put into his mouth, he asks for a drink of water while on the electric chair after quoting, "Ich aß und wurde nicht satt, ich trank und wurde durstig."[3] Brecht even has the hero commend Jenny to his last friend Heinrich while awaiting execution, in an evocation of the scene of Mary and St. John under the Cross (Jn 19:26–27).[4]

The question then emerges as Paul Ackermann asks his executioners, the Mahagonny people, if they don't realize that there is a God: "Ihr wißt wohl nicht, daß es einen Gott gibt?" (GW, II, 558). The answer that Begbick gives is a curious bit of Brechtian "theology." First the question is reinterpreted by Begbick into whether or not there is a God *for us in Mahagonny*. "Ach so, ob es für uns einen Gott gibt?" (GW, II, 558). Although the following *Spiel von Gott in Mahagonny* confirms an ironic belief in the existence of hell (the city), and in theophanies in Mahagonny that are a function of whiskey, the *Spiel* is really a clever avoidance of the question about God that was in Paul's mind. Begbick and Trinity-Moses have decided to "make it" down here and so they really neither hear nor any longer pay any attention to the type of question asked by people who "eat but don't get full, drink and remain thirsty." Brecht has thus managed to keep the question about God asked by dying men unanswered, and yet allows the Mahagonny people to give the answer they have ready about God in the City! Dramatically, Brecht is able to have Begbick and Moses stage their mocking play on the *absence* of God in Mahagonny with the bitterly powerful visual irony of having the performance done in the presence of An Innocent Man. He is not recognized by them and they execute him as he says again the "I thirst" of the Passion, "Gebt mir doch ein Glas Wasser!" (GW, II, 561). To him only the vinegar of the Passion account can be offered along with Veronica's face cloth. Even the pincers are present, traditional instruments of the removal of the nails, for the lowering of the corpse. As the corpse is lifted in procession the men sing:

> Können ihm Essig holen
> Können sein Gesicht abreiben
> Können die Beißzange holen
> . . .
> Können einem toten Mann nicht helfen. (GW, II, 563)

Though it may seem dramatically and religiously inconsistent to have the execution carried out by Trinity-Moses, I think his involvement renders the scene all the more powerful. Execution at the hands of the religious authorities is not inconsistent with what Brecht wants to say about Net City nor is it inconsistent with the Passion. The name "Trinity-Moses" may also indicate something of Brecht's purpose. Logically, the founder of Mahagonny who is called Trinity-Moses, if he represents the collusion of Judaeo-Christianity with capitalistic economics, probably should have been named "Jesus-Moses," after the two chief personifications of the Two Testaments. "God-Moses" would not incorporate both of the traditions, and would not be artificial enough to be taken with any equanimity by the audience. "Trinity" is just theologically academic enough to be possible and acceptable to the audience. This device makes it theatrically possible to have a stuffed-shirt character, who is able to represent the double Judaeo-Christian tradition, as participating in the corruption of the West, and yet still separate Jesus and his death from the character of Trinity-Moses. Brecht is thus able to use the Passion of Christ and the sympathy it will gain in connection with Paul Ackermann. Keeping the name of Jesus out of the Christian half of the Trinity-Moses character will give the audience even more chance to see the innate but invisible cruelty of such "bourgeois" mottoes as "Wie man sich bettet, so liegt man" in the moment when it is sung to the execution of Brecht's Paul. Christ can thus be used against the "Christianity" of business people in the city, as he was used against "the Bible" in *Die Bibel*. In addition to all this, one also gets the distinct feeling that for Brecht, regardless of his belief or non-belief in God, and his antagonism to the organized church, the death of Jesus is somehow a sacred event, an archetype for him of the mystery of the death of the good man.

The following brief commentary may help the reader identify some of the main allusions made by Brecht in the course of *Mahagonny*.

Table 3

Mahagonny	*The Bible*
Sc. 1: Die Wüste; wir müssen umkehren.	The Exodus, the grumbling in the desert against Moses.
von Angesicht zu Angesicht	playing with liturgical formula "von Ewigkeit zu Ewigkeit."
Darum laßt uns hier eine Stadt gründen Und sie nennen Mahagonny Das heißt: Netzestadt!	Conglomerate of biblical language from Genesis (Gen 1:26—Und Gott sprach: Laßt uns Menschen machen) and from the New Testament usage of explaining strange names, e.g., Mt 1:23—Und sie nannte ihn Emmanuel, das heißt: Gott mit uns; or Eli, Eli, . . . das ist: Mein Gott, Mein Gott, . . . Etc.—the city of Jerusalem founded after the Exodus.

Table 3 (*continued*)

Wie ein Netz für die Vögel	Eccl 9:12—Auch weiß der Mensch seine Zeit nicht, sondern wie die Fische gefangen werden, so werden auch die Menschen verstrickt zur bösen Zeit, wenn sie plötzlich über sie fällt.
Und eine Woche ist hier: sieben Tage ohne Arbeit	Brecht's Mahagonnian reversal of the seven Days of Creation, c.f. Gen 2:2— Und so vollendete Gott am siebenten Tage seine Werke, die er machte, und ruhte am siebenten Tage von allen seinen Werken, die er gemacht hatte.
Sc. 3: Paradiesstadt Unter unsern Städten	Eden. liturgical; the scene is set up so that this "psalm" to nihilism is recited in almost traditional psalmody, with "die Männer" acting as choir for the antiphon at beginning and end, and with Moses and Willy alternatingly reciting the "psalm." Weill's music expresses this perfectly.
Sc. 5: Damals kam unter anderen auch Paul Ackermann in die Stadt Mahagonny.	Lk 2:3–4—Und jedermann ging, . . . ein jeglicher in seine Stadt. Da machte sich auf auch Joseph . . . zur Stadt Davids
Sc. 8: Alle wahrhaft Suchenden werden enttäuscht.	against Mt 7:7—suchet, so werdet ihr finden.
Wunderbar ist das Heraufkommen des Abends Und schön sind die Gespräche der Männer unter sich! Schön ist die Ruhe und der Frieden Und beglückend ist die Eintracht. Herrlich ist das einfache Leben Und ohnegleichen ist die Größe der Natur.	This is free recreation in the Hebrew Psalm form, in which each second line is expected to parallel the first. Weill, of course, put it to harmonized psalmody. Satirizes petit bourgeois contentment, with a little sympathy.

Table 3 (*continued*)

Und es ist immer noch nichts geschehn. Oh, Jungens, es ist immer noch nichts geschehn!	Eccl 1:9–10 & 14 & *passim*. Und es geschieht nichts Neues unter der Sonne. Weill's music uses Bach Chorale-type intonations for "Oh, Jungens."
Sc. 9: Als die Zeit vorbei war	biblical time formula, e.g., Lk 2:6 & 9:51—da die Zeit erfüllet war. Usually to indicate the beginning of a new event—here used mockingly of the coming to Mahagonny after 7 years of work (7 years, like 40 days, is also a biblical time cliché for "a long time").
Sc. 10: Wo ist eine Mauer, die mich verbirgt? Wo ist eine Höhle, die mich aufnimmt?	Free creation in the psalmic form; the content is from the popular preaching tradition on the helplessness of the sinner when the Judgment comes.
Sc. 11: Haltet euch aufrecht, fürchtet euch nicht Was hilft alles Klagen Dem, der gegen Hurrikane ficht?	in the tone of the Eschatological Discourse of Jesus in Mk 13 on the end of world: Sehet zu, daß euch nicht jemand verführe! . . . Es werden Erdbeben geschehen . . . fürchtet euch nicht! (cf. *Die Bibel*, Scene 2, where the same section of Mark is used in the same context of the threatened end of a city!) Weill's music alludes to Bach.
Wo immer du hingehst Es nützt nichts.	a very nihilistic reversal of the famous reply of Ruth (Ruth 1:16)—Wo du hingehest, da will ich auch gehen; wo du bleibst, da bleibe ich auch, etc. (also used exactly as in Ruth 1:16 in *Die Dreigroschenoper*).
Was eben ist, das muß krumm werden Und was hoch ragt, das muß in den Staub.	Lk 3:5, reversed by Brecht: . . . und was krumm ist, soll richtig werden (b) . . . und alle Berge und Hügel sollen erniedrigt werden (a) . . . und was uneben ist, soll ebener Weg werden (c).

Table 3 (*continued*)

(Paul to Begbick) Siehst du, du hast Tafeln gemacht Und darauf geschrieben: Das ist verboten Und dieses darfst du nicht.	Moses and the Ten Commandments (also used in *Puntila*).[5] Ex 19–20. Here, interestingly enough, spoken not to Trinity-Moses, as one would expect, but to the power behind him, the widow Begbick.
Aber noch vor es zwei schlägt Werde ich, Paul Ackermann Singen, was lustig ist . . .	Peter's Denial.[6] Mt 26:34—Und Jesus sprach zu ihm: . . . ich sage dir, heute in dieser Nacht ehe der Hahn zweimal krähet, wirst du mich dreimal ver- leugnen. (Also used in *Baal*, *Edward II*, and *Mutter Courage*.)
Laßt euch nicht verführen . . . Ihr sterbt mit allen Tieren Und es kommt nichts nachher.	Mk 13, Eschatological Discourse, as above, combined again (as in *Baal*) with man-animal identification in death from Eccl 3:18–21—. . . Denn es geht dem Menschen wie dem Vieh: wie dies stirbt, so stirbt auch er, und sie haben alle einen Odem, und der Mensch hat nichts voraus vor dem Vieh; denn es ist alles eitel. Weill's music reemphasizes the biblicality of this nihilism by putting it in the chorale mode reminiscent of the *St. Matthew's Passion*.
zerschlage lieber deine Tafeln	Ex 32:19—Als Mose aber nahe zum Lager kam . . . entbrannte sein Zorn, und er warf die Tafeln aus der Hand und zerbrach sie unten am Berge.
Und untergehen die Gerechten mit den Ungerechten. (Begbick, when she hears of the destruction of Pensacola by the hurricane)	Nihilistic reversal of Mt 5:45—Liebet eure Feinde, auf daß ihr Kinder seid eures Vaters im Himmel. Denn er läßt seine Sonne aufgehen über die Bösen und über die Guten und läßt regnen über Gerechte und Ungerechte. (Brecht's change is significant. He removes a text from the moral realm— charity—and by looking from the point of view of death changes it into

Table 3 (*continued*)

	an eschatological or apocalyptic one, relativizing good and bad not by relating them to an absolute God, but by relating them to the absolute in the play: death.)
Sc. 13–16: (*Essen Lieben Kämpfen Saufen*)	(The capital sins of *Mahagonny*, each one personified as in a morality play, each one ending in death.)
Sc. 18: (The Trial)	There is a similarity of situation between the trial of Christ by the High Priest and Sanhedrin, and the trial of Paul by Trinity-Moses and the men of Mahagonny; the abandonment of Paul by his friends (this is more clearly biblical in the parallel scene of *Baal*); the innocence of the accused, etc. Brecht, however, alludes directly to none of the commonplaces of the trial of Christ, such as the High Priest's rending of his garments, etc., but instead creates the tone of the biblical situation through the above, reinforced by Weill's liberal use of Bach. Cf. especially the Chorale of the men of Mahagonny singing "Er hat kein Geld . . . Nieder mit ihm!" from St. Matthew's Passion, and by the position of the trial before the events and allusions to the rest of the Passion in the following scene, 19.
Erhebt sich der Schrei nach Sühne.	the "sins that cry to heaven for vengeance"—a bitter application of the worst category of sins in moral theology to the situation of not having any money, based on Cain's murder of Abel, Gen 4:10—Die Stimme des Blutes deines Bruders schreit zu mir von der Erde.

Table 3 *(continued)*

Sc. 19: Paul's commending of Jenny to his last friend, Heinrich, prior to his execution: Und jetzt empfehle ich dich/Meinem letzten Freund Heinrich.	Christ's commending of Mary into his beloved disciple's care, during the crucifixion. Jn 19:26–27—Da nun Jesus seine Mutter sah und den Jünger dabeistehen, den er liebhatte, spricht er zu seiner Mutter: "Weib, siehe, das ist dein Sohn." . . . Und von der Stunde an, nahm sie der Jünger zu sich. (The reader may notice that both this incident and the *Sitio* below have been taken from juxtaposed texts in John's Gospel.)
Ich aß und wurde nicht satt, ich trank und wurde durstig.	Paul Ackermann's dissociation from the "religion of self-satisfaction" of Mahagonny. Brecht has combined two separate biblical citations (from the Feeding of the Five Thousand and the Woman at the Well), reversed them by changing *sie* to *ich*, then conflated them in the best biblical manner. Mt 15:20—Und sie aßen alle und wurden satt. Jn 4:14—(Jesus antwortete und sprach zu ihr): Wer von diesem Wasser trinkt, den wird wieder dürsten; (wer aber von dem Wasser trinken wird, das ich ihm gebe, den wird ewiglich nicht dürsten . . .).
Gebt mir doch ein Glas Wasser	*Sitio.* Jn 19:28—Mich dürstet, (after the mocking *Spiel von Gott*), in reply to the condemned man's question: "Ihr wißt wohl nicht, daß es einen Gott gibt?"
Sc. 20: As the corpse of Paul Ackermann is borne in the 5th procession: Können ihm Essig holen / Können sein Gesicht abreiben / Können die Beißzange holen	Jn 19:29–30—Da stand ein Gefäß voll Essig. Sie aber füllten einen Schwamm mit Essig und steckten ihn auf einen Ysop und hielten es ihm dar zum Munde. (The wiping of the face, Veronica's Veil, and the pincers for the deposition from the Cross, are com-

Table 3 *(continued)*

monly depicted along with the Cross
in German churches along with the
crown, nails, and the other instruments of the Passion. The text of Jn
19:29 immediately follows the two
used above in Scene 19.)

From this short commentary a certain insight can be obtained into
the aesthetics of Brecht's use of biblical allusion. Brecht does not so
much use quotational allusion (it is often very difficult to locate any
exact word-for-word source for his biblical statements) or even personal allusion—Trinity-Moses is not made to climb any mountains,
nor is there any serious attempt to identify him in a personal way
with the Moses of Mt. Sinai; Paul Ackermann is not made into such a
literal Christ-figure that he cannot also be made to speak words said
by St. Peter during the Passion. Rather, Brecht uses a kind of situational allusion. Just as Brecht freely imitates the sound and tone of the
Bible in statements entirely his own, so he also freely uses biblical
situations for his own ends. In this way it is the Exodus-situation that
is evoked in the first scene to be travestied, and although this requires
a sort of Moses to be present and requires allusions to the "turning
back" statements in the Bible, it is the suggestion of the Exodus-
situation that is primarily being used. This is an evocative rather than
dramatic use of the Bible. "Evocative" here means suggestive usage
rather than precisely impositional, as in the manner of a preacher. It
is a deliberate dialectical usage which creates a taut relationship between the ancient biblical situation and the modern parallel situation
in the play, and it eschews a simple, point for point representation of
the biblical situation on the stage in a too easily recognized parallel
form. This evocative use is also exemplified in the second important
biblical situation in *Mahagonny*, the crisis of the coming of the *Taifun*
in Scenes 10 and 11. The eschatological or apocalyptic situation of
these scenes does not allude to any specific personal events in the
Bible, but is rather a conglomerate of *apocalyptica* from the New Testament on the end of the world and/or the fall of the city of Jerusalem,
combined with the techniques and jargon of modern hurricane re-
porting.

The third biblical situation used in Mahagonny is the Passion and
Death. The Passion appears in an "evocative" manner, primarily
through similarity of situation: it is night, an authority with religious
title is the trial judge, the accused commends the woman to his last

friend, and vinegar is brought to drink. It is reinforced through two indirect quotations: the request for a glass of water and the "I commend you to my last friend, Henry"; and the parallel of the abandonment of Paul Ackermann to the *Verlassenheit* of Christ on the Cross. Brecht seems to be saying that in the death of the kind or good person in the city it is not so much that Jesus Christ is again dying in such a person, but rather than in such a *situation*, the *situation* of Calvary is happening again. For this, it is as necessary that the prepetrators of the act be as unaware of what they are doing as were the perpetrators then. But the audience does feel that something is wrong, and, due to Brecht's situational method of allusion, they can be drawn into great sympathy with the hero without quite realizing why. This is far more powerful drama than if Brecht were to have Paul Ackermann come out with a "Father, forgive them, for they know not what they do," or some other direct quotation which would immediately alienate all but the simplest of audiences, and would not inspire a subterranean desire to change the *situation* that causes such deaths.

Brecht's displeasure with the values of Net City are expresseed in the curious reason given for the abandonment of Paul by his friends: money. The amount of money involved is a clue to the underlying form of *Mahagonny*. The price for the three bottles of whiskey and a curtain rod might come to about $20. People are paying $5 to see the trial. We are clearly outside the realm of naturalistic drama and realistic plot. Using a small amount of money in this didactic way brings *Mahagonny* into the realm of the parable. The death of Paul Ackermann in *Mahagonny* is a parable on the old theme of money as "the root of all evil," a parable on the consequences of serving Mammon (money) by an author who cannot say the traditional "you cannot serve both God and Mammon" and who therefore says you cannot serve both kindness and Mammon.

Brecht pictures both the founders and inhabitants of Mahagonny as people who are afraid "weil es nichts gibt, woran man sich halten kann" (GW, II, 503). The "nothing" that they are afraid of, is the nonexistence that comes when you have to sustain yourself in life, when "Jeder Beliebige könnte mich in den Straßengraben schubsen" (GW, IV, 1389). People whom you could trust when your existence was not in question, you cannot call upon when it is. Brecht thus posits again as a common reality of the marketplace and everyday life the old Thomistic distinction between essence and existence, and, like the Thomists, asserts the priority of existence over essence in the concrete circumstances of human life on this planet. Jenny is not afraid to give Paul her love, and Heinrich is not afraid to admit to Paul "du stehst mir menschlich nahe," but because of a far greater fear he feels obliged to add, "aber Geld ist eine andre Sache." Love is the highest quality of man's essence, but it can do little to continue his existence when the latter is threatened. Love enables man to be what he really is, but money enables that same man to be—and he must first be, before he can love. As is said so often in *Die Dreigroschenoper,* "Erst kommt das Fressen, dann kommt die Moral!" (GW, II, 457). Translated into theological language: existence precedes essence.

Brecht's "negative theology" rests on the fear of nonexistence (death) overcoming man's essence: love. He posits this fear of "nothing" as the reason for the very founding of city life and the reason for its continuance. Theologically, he posits the fear of death as the origin of the problem of evil. He thus has two distinct types of human weakness to present on the stage and not just one: the first is the human weakness of Leokadja Begbick and all the inhabitants of Mahagonny, a weakness rooted in the metaphysical fear of not having anything with which to hold off the coming of nonexistence, the coming of night, death, and chaos. It is no accident that Begbick's successor, the protagonist of *Mutter Courage,* will be called Anna Fierling [*scil.* fear-ling], a name that contradicts her public title and exposes her inner self. This fear of nonexistence is best alleviated by selling. Selling aids in the acquisition of money, which in turn helps keep death and social impotence at arm's length. Selling pleasures to men also assuages their fear and boredom by providing some transitory excitement and temporary relief from the peaceful but ominous "Heraufkommen des Abends."

The second type of human weakness is the constant temptation to put human essence (charity, *Mitleid,* loving) before the priority of one's own existence. If this temptation is not resisted, then one will not succeed in this world, one will end up losing one's existence for one's essence. This "mistake" (which the New Testament counsels all to make), a mistake that Brecht loves, was made by the *Vater* in *Die Bibel,* the drowned girl in *Baal,* and by Paul Ackermann. It will be made as well by Kattrin and by Grusche. Every time someone loses his or her life out of love by betting on a friend, Brecht will be reminded, as is the *Feldprediger* in *Mutter Courage,* of the Crucifixion, and of how we have made this world a place where love costs one's existence in it. He also implies that anyone so sacrificing himself is following the example of Christ, but, despite all this, Brecht will not say, "welche Dummheiten er glaubt" nor will he affirm the possibility of a God beyond "der blaue Himmel." For, if "über ihm [dem Himmel] ist nichts" (GW, II, 576), then such noble human sympathy is only a quicker entering into nothingness for the self-sacrificing person. And we are reminded of the ending of *Mahagonny*: "Können einem toten Mann nicht helfen."

Perhaps this corroborates the pattern of the use of the Passion and Death that we have seen in the plays so far, for if the only real absolute in Brecht's thought is death, and the model person with whom he chooses to identify his "good" characters is Christ, then the most perfect artistic synthesis of these two would be Jesus-in-death. Jesus in death, however, is the Crucifixion, and the Passion and Death becomes the ideal vehicle for Brecht's thought on the fate of the good person in this world. Still, it is Jesus Crucified and Him Dead that Brecht preaches, which is a far more tragic "faith" than the Jesus Crucified who "if he has not risen your faith is vain" of St. Paul (1 Cor 15:17). Brecht's parable of Paul Ackermann preaches Religious Nihilism.

Brecht's anger in this parable, however, is not directed solely at the evil of nonexistence. Net City is also a parable against the evils of the *essence* of the *condition humaine*, a description of men's self-inflicted trappedness in their own nets, a deploring of the inability of men to help one another *before* they die, expressed in a more heightened way by pointing out the absolute futility of attempting such help afterwards. The awful irony in Scene 16 of Jenny professing her love for Paul without ever realizing that she could save him by risking some of her existence (money) on him, brings even love into question as a real bond between people. She and his best friend Heinrich could communally give the $20 at $10 apiece, one is tempted to suggest, thereby avoiding the good-bye love scene, and saving Heinrich his brilliant oratory (and no money) on Paul's behalf. But they are too afraid to be teachable, they do not realize that what they are doing contributes to Paul's death, just as Mother Courage never comes to the realization that her very business is contributing to her children's deaths. They are too afraid to recognize that they could combine existences as well as essences in a communism of money. Because of her blind unwillingness Jenny goes from being a lover to a widow; she becomes another widow Begbick. Paul, giving his "Mary" and "John" to each other, saying "I ate and was not filled, I drank and remained thirsty," with the sad implication that there was something entirely different from all this life that he had been longing for, dies in thirst in *Mahagonny*.[7] And as he dies the inhabitants put on their "God-Play" on life in Mahagonny as hell. "Und es kommt nichts nachher."

The journey of modern man in his Exodus from the country to the city has not ended in the founding of a New Jerusalem. Miami is no Paradise regained, the "moon of Alabama" is no substitute for the one made on the Third Day, the joys of the big city leave the Paul Ackermanns still hungry and still thirsty for something else. No alternative is proposed by Brecht. The last lines seem to imply that any alternative would just end up producing more of the same. This is almost explicitly said in the earlier version of the play in the Benares-song in which the Mahagonnians contemplate trying to find another place to go to where all would be well. Brecht has come to the very serious problem of whether or not it is worthwhile preaching against man's inhumanity to man. Why protest the present condition of things if the future condition can be no better? Brecht's communism should have given him an answer, but in most plays one suspects (as opposed to his private speeches) his communism is absent as a solution and seems mainly to be a "Benares," not that much different from Mahagonny, to which we attempt to flee in face of the oncoming enemy. The reason for this lies, no doubt, in what Brecht sees as the real enemy: death. The real enemy is always present and at the end of *Mahagonny*, as at the end of *Baal*, enters in to terminate the proceedings in the place of any solution on the level of essence. Paul Ackermann's death, as a death in a parable, can be taken as a moral death, the living death of having nothing and yet still being biologically alive in a city, but it is even more than that. The procession carrying his corpse around is once again warning of the absolute futility, Ecclesiastes's *Eitelkeit*, that makes the whole intolerable situation of *Mahagonny* possible, as well as any attempt to reform it futile: death. One can crusade and march in demonstrations for the poor or the rich, the capitalist or the communist; the widow, the orphan, the resident alien, but once someone is dead no human help is worth anything. There, *die Moral* is of no help whatsoever, nor can it provide any real reason for having worried one way or the other about one's fellow man while one was still alive. "Können einem toten Mann nicht helfen./Können uns und euch und niemand helfen."

And yet Brecht is concerned. In Brecht there is the conflict of the Prophet and the Wisdom writer of Ecclesiastes. He does protest the bad treatment of the weak and the poor, while seeing in death the demonstration that "all is vain, and a chasing after the wind." With the coming of World War II, the conflict between these two parts of himself breaks out in what may be his most successful and most beautiful work, *Mutter Courage und ihre Kinder*.

V

Mutter Courage und ihre Kinder: To Save or Not to Save the City Besieged

About ten years after Mahagonny, Brecht wrote *Mutter Courage und ihre Kinder*. The nemesis that threatens his heroine and her children is no longer primarily the biological death of *Baal*, nor the financial death of *Mahagonny*, but rather the death of *Die Bibel*, military-ideological death, death-in-war. It seems clear that just as biology and his experience as an orderly were the main influences on Brecht's *Baal*, and Marxist analysis of capitalism was preponderant in *Mahagonny*, World War II (and his having to flee into exile) was dominant in *Mutter Courage*.

In the years between *Mahagonny* and *Mutter Courage*, 1929–1939, Brecht's drama reflects serious concern both with communism and its call for the tragic self-sacrifice of the individual (*Badener Lehrstück vom Einverständnis, Der Jasager, Die Maßnahme*) and with fascism, with its accompanying sacrifice of the weak and the poor (*Furcht und Elend des Dritten Reichs*—originally entitled *Deutschland—ein Greuelmärchen, Das Verhör des Lukullus*). His hasty flight from Germany after the Nazis came to power in 1933 is well-known.[1] By way of Prague, Zurich, and Paris he eventually came to Denmark where he stayed first on the Island of Thurö, at the invitation of the Danish writer Karin Michaelis, and then on the nearby Island of Fünen near Svendborg. There, in a place where he could continue to hear radio broadcasts every day from Germany, he continued to write on a table set up in a whitewashed stable.[2]

Brecht's relationship to institutional communism seems also to have taken a more serious turn during this critical period of 1938–39, a turn that may have allowed him the greater objectivity toward this and all ideologies that is reflected in *Mutter Courage*. Brecht had to face up to what communism could do under Stalin by way of ruthless repression:

Of the three Russian friends whom he [Brecht] had approached in March, 1937, with a view to forming an international "Diderot Society" of like-minded theatre people, within a matter of weeks Eisenstein had been denounced in Pravda and stopped working on Bezhin Meadow, Okhlopkhov had lost his theatre, and Tretiakov had been arrested and shot. . . . By the middle of 1937 Kun and Knorin, the two Comintern members who had shown themselves friendly to him in Moscow in 1935, had been arrested and tortured, while one of his leading actresses, Carola Neher, had been arrested with her Russian husband and sentenced to ten years' hard labor on an espionage charge; all three were later killed.[3]

Finding atrocities on both sides, both in capitalism under Hitler and in communism under Stalin, set the mental stage for an isolation from absolutist economic ideologies and for a searching back in the roots of his thought for an attitude toward ideologies that Brecht had had as a teenager when he wrote *Die Bibel*. Willet and Manheim comment further on what effect the communist (as well as the Nazi) atrocities were having on the author who had abandoned the neutralist, humanist position of *Die Bibel* for the *engagé*, partisan position of *Mahagonny*:

Such horrifying developments within Brecht's own camp combined with the unchecked progress of the Nazi enemy (e.g., the swallowing of Austria in the spring of 1938), to bring a new element of sadness into his work. Thus Walter Benjamin, who arrived in Brecht's village [on Fünen] at the end of June 1938 when Tretiakov's probable fate had become clear, . . . found that his friend seemed to have got much less prickly and provocative and interprets this in a letter to Theodor Adorno as a sign of his growing isolation.[4]

Though most seem to date Brecht's first serious difficulties with institutional communism from his last period in East Berlin, especially in connection with the Russian-suppressed revolt of the workers in 1953, still the poet Brecht seems to have realized the problem of the individual under communism almost from the beginning, as for example, in *Die Maßnahme*, or in the secret poems of 1938–39, of which Manheim and Willett write: "It was what Brecht in his verse of 1938–39 calls 'the dark times,' a 'bad time for poetry': a kind of paralyzed horror fills the poems which he then wrote about Neher and Tretiakov and which remained unpublished until after his death."[5]

Nonetheless, it was precisely this isolation and this "bad time" for political poetry that might be too dangerously specific that produced the mental ambience which enabled the inspiration of *Die Bibel* to blossom again, though in a new and powerfully tragic form: Mother Europe at war again, killing her children for survival and profit at the behest of conflicting ideologies—the Thirty Years' War, World War II;

the "Catholics" versus the "Protestants," the Allies versus Germany, communism versus capitalism. The common man lets himself be enticed once again into the service of the strong in a mistaken attempt to gain strength, and ends up, as the weak always do in Brecht, sacrificed to the strong and to their ambitions. Brecht thus sets out again to warn the weak, and to expose the strong.

In the midst of the isolation and personal agony of having to question communism, which he thought had brought some meaning and "salvation" to his life, and having to regard it, too, as one more violent contender for power over people, one that will rely on strength just as much as will Begbick and Trinity-Moses, Brecht reverts to his childhood support of the opposed mentality: weakness, the Father in *Die Bibel*. The common man, weak, unable to understand the Emperor's great plans for "protecting" ever more of Poland, seeking only a little beer and company, becomes the antihero to the "heroic" generals of the war.

Human weakness, the temptation to help one's fellow man, to feel pity and because of that to risk money and/or one's existence for the sake of one's essence, love, resulted in *Mahagonny* in a) execution, and b) no help rendered. Now, ten years later, there comes, out of compassion for fighting Europe, the first great change in Brecht's "moral theology" of weakness. The "Können uns und euch und niemand helfen" of *Mahagonny*'s final chorus is changed in *Mutter Courage* to the cannon of the besieged city responding, finally, to the last drumbeats of Kattrin's death: "Können jemand helfen!" The weak can sometimes help the weak. Brecht does not indeed change his constant theme that the weak-good will be crucified, but he seems to alter his opinion about whether or not their compassion can help the city. Later, in *Der gute Mensch von Sezuan*, he will modify this further, resolving the issue in terms of the paradox of the good person being forced also to be ruthless on occasion. And the gods are not able to give any real answer as to why it is necessary for those who live in their Creation to have to be both "gentle as doves and wise as serpents" in order to survive there.

In another play written in this same crucial time, 1938–39, Brecht makes weakness itself into the condition for justification. During his trial in the land of the shades, General Lucullus in *Das Verhör des Lukullus* tries to rest his case on his great achievements during Rome's wars. During the course of the trial it turns out that all he seems to have accomplished for mankind is the losing of mothers' sons. He then accuses the court of not understanding war. One witness, *das Fischweib*, in her testimony summarizes the argument of the whole play and is subsequently acknowledged by the court as having a real

understanding of war. Since both war and the mother's relation to
her offspring are so important to Mutter Courage, we will cite most of
her argument here. In her speech the *Fischweib* calls her son by a
name whose subsequent usage in the poem once again suggests
Brecht's "theology" of the repetition of the crucifixion (we will return
to this theme again in connection with Schweizerkas and the *Feldprediger*):

> Ich verstehe ihn [den Krieg]. Mein Sohn
> Ist im Kriege gefallen.
> Ich war Fischweib auf dem Markt am Forum.
> Eines Tages hieß es, daß die Schiffe
> Der Zurückgekommnen aus dem Asienkriege
> Eingelaufen sei'n. Ich lief vom Markte
> Und ich stand am Tiber viele Stunden
> Wo sie ausgebootet wurden, und am Abend
> Waren alle Schiffe leer. Mein Sohn war
> Über ihre Planken nicht gekommen.
> Da es zugig war am Hafen, fiel ich
> Nachts in Fieber, und im Fieber suchte
> Ich nun meinen Sohn, und tiefer suchend
> Fror ich mehr, und dann, gestorben, kam ich
> Hier ins Schattenreich und suchte weiter.
> Faber, rief ich, denn das war sein Name.
> Faber, mein Sohn Faber
> Den ich trug und den ich aufzog
> Mein Sohn Faber!
> Und ich lief und lief durch Schatten
> Und vorbei an Schatten hin zu Schatten
> Faber rufend, bis ein Pförtner drüben
> In den Lagern der im Krieg Gefallnen
> Mich am Ärmel einhielt und mir sagte:
> Alte, hier sind viele Faber. . . .[6]

In view of this testimony, the judge becomes even more annoyed at
Lucullus's constant reliance on his power and his victories for acquit-
tal, and in the climax finally says to him:

> Erzürne uns lieber nicht weiter mit deinen Triumphen.
> Hast du keine Zeugen
> Für irgendeine Schwäche, Mensch?
> Deine Sache steht ungünstig. Deine Tugenden
> Scheinen wenig nützlich, vielleicht
> Ließen deine Schwächen Lücken

In der Kette der Gewalttaten?
Entsinne dich deiner Schwächen
Schatte, ich rat es dir. (GW, IV, 1473)

In the outline commentary which follows, the reader will be able to see once again not only the reemergence of the Judith myth (as Brecht uses it), but also his use of the Crucifixion and Death to establish a figurative framework within which to understand both the death of Schweizerkas in Scene 3 and the death of Kattrin in Scene 11. In neither death is the Bible used in an alienating way; in both cases it is used empathetically, both to identify the situation of the death as the ever-recurring death of the innocent weak, and to cause audience sympathy. The Bible is, of course, also used to attain estrangement throughout the play, for example, in Scene 2 with the *Feldhauptmann*, and in the first part of Scene 3. In addition to his use of the Matthew Passion account, Brecht falls back as well on his commonplaces from Ecclesiastes, Isaiah, and Genesis.

Table 4

Mutter Courage	*The Bible*
Sc. 1: Ihr solltet . . . Jakob Ochs und Esau Ochs heißen, . . .	Gen 25:21–34. Esau and Jacob were twin sons of Isaac and Rebecca. The allusion here seems to be purely verbal, although it does suggest family.
Ich, schmerzensreiche Gebärerin (Mutter Courage)	Mother of Sorrows, popular Catholic devotion to the sorrows of Mary, frequently depicted as the Pietà, based on Simeon's prophecy to Mary during the Presentation in the temple, Lk 2:35. Also familiar through Goethe's use as Gretchen's prayer: Ach, neige, du Schmerzensreiche . . .
ein Kreuz steht auch über deinem Weg (Mutter Courage)	similar in tone and content to Lk 2:35 above . . . Und auch durch deine Seele wird ein Schwert dringen. It is masterful that Brecht, who is so anxious that the plot be given away in advance, uses in Scene 1 that part of the Gospel to give it away in which the evangelist himself is giving away (or "prophesying") what the end of Jesus will be at the hands of

Table 4 *(continued)*

	men. It provides a gentle poetic "setting up" of the "pietà" of the first part of the last scene of the play, as well as the crucifixion-death of Kattrin.
Sc. 2: Nun, mein Sohn, herein mit dir zu deinem Feldhauptmann und setz dich zu meiner Rechten. (Feldhauptmann to Eilif)	"to sit at the right hand," biblical commonplace for being honored, usually by the Divine, e.g., Acts 7:55 (Stephanus) sah Jesus zur Rechten Gottes; Mk 16:19—(Jesus) setzte sich zur rechten Hand Gottes, etc. Here used ironically.
[Wir sind gekommen, ihnen ihre Seelen zu retten, . . . (Feldhauptmann)]	[cf. *Die Bibel*, outline commentary, p. 21].
'Not kennt kein Gebot' nicht? . . . in der Bibel steht der Satz nicht, aber unser Herr hat aus fünf Broten fünfhundert herzaubern können . . . da konnt er auch verlangen, daß man seinen Nächsten liebt, denn man war satt. Heutzutage ist das anders. (Feldprediger)	Mt 14:17–20—Und er nahm die fünf Brote, . . . gab die Brote den Jüngern, und die Jünger gaben sie dem Volk. Und sie aßen alle und wurden satt. . . . Mt 22:39—Du sollst deinen Nächsten lieben wie dich selbst. Brecht's juxtaposition makes the miracle of loaves the precondition for the practical validity of the Second Great Commandment (Love thy neighbor as thyself.) Erst kommt das Fressen, *dann* die Moral.
Ihr vergeht wie der Rauch! Und die Wärme geht auch	Nonexistence warning in terms of smoke, from Hosea 13:3, as well as Isaiah and Ecclesiastes, as already used in other plays, cf. outline commentary on *Baal*, pp. 42–44.
Sc. 3: Der ist nicht seinem Bruder sein Zahlmeister. Er soll ihn nicht in Versuchung führen. . . .	possible Brecht adjustment of Cain's reply to God in the Cain and Abel story (Gen 4:9—Soll ich meines Bruders Hüter sein?) combined with the second last petition of the Lord's Prayer, Mt 3:13—Und führe uns nicht in Versuchung—thereby making one's brother be the origin of temptation!

Table 4 *(continued)*

Es ist ein Glaubenskrieg . . . und also Gott wohlgefällig.	bitter use of the concept of "holy war" reinforced with the biblical "wohlgefällig," e.g., Rom 12:1—heilig und Gott wohlgefällig; Prüfet, was da sei wohlgefällig dem Herrn—Eph 5:10, etc., cf. *Die Bibel.*
Selig sind die Friedfertigen, heißts im Krieg.	the seventh Beatitude, Mt 5:9, ironically treated.
. . . diese Babylonische. (Mutter Courage to Kattrin)	the whore of Babylon, i.e., epitome of sinfulness, cf. Acts 17:5.
Sein Licht muß man unter den Scheffel stellen, heißt es. (Mutter Courage to Feldprediger as she smears dirt on Kattrin when the Catholics come.)	Reversal of the biblical counsel given in Mt 5:15 (man zündet nicht ein Licht an, und setzt es unter einen Scheffel) due to "the way things are."
Wes das Herz voll ist, des läuft das Maul über, heißts, aber weh, wenns mir überläuft! (Feldprediger)	Mt 12:34, with a slight Brecht alteration of Mund to Maul, and with the accompanying humorous denial of the truth of the citation in the chaplain's actual situation.
Wir sind eben jetzt in Gottes Hand (Feldprediger). Ich glaub nicht, daß wir schon so verloren sind. (Mutter Courage)	Wis 3:1—der Gerechten Seelen sind in Gottes Hand.—Humorously ironic handling of a preacher's commonplace.
"armes Tier" (to Kattrin by Schweizerkas)	Cf. outline commentary on Brecht's possible use of animal imagery from Ecclesiastes in *Baal*, pp. 42–44, and *Mahagonny*, p. 60, as well as *die Bäuerin*'s address to Kattrin in Scene 11 of *Mutter Courage*. This common phrase, "armes Tier," is used by Brecht to express human weakness.
Wollt ihr etwa tun, als kennt ihr ihn nicht? (Feldwebel). Wie soll ich ihn kennen? (Mutter Courage)	Mt 26:69–75, Peter's Denial, suggested by situational allusion . . . Und er leugnete abermals und schwur dazu: Ich kenne den Menschen nicht. [Cf. outline commentary to *Mahagonny*, p. 60, note.]

Table 4 *(continued)*

Er ist ganz ordentlich gesessen und hat das Maul nicht aufgemacht, . . .	allusion to the commonplace scriptural comparison of Christ's sufferings to that of the lamb that does not open its mouth when being taken to the slaughter. Taken from Isaiah's description of the Suffering Servant: [Als er gemartert ward, litt er doch willig] und tat seinen Mund nicht auf, wie ein Lamm, das zur Schlachtbank geführt wird. Is 53:7.
Solche Fäll . . . sind in der Religionsgeschicht nicht unbekannt [referring to all the above with Schweizerkas]. Ich erinner an die Passion von unserm Herrn und Heiland. (Feldprediger)	"Ich erinner an die Passion"— Matthew's Passion, most probably. Reflects Brecht's attitude on the relationship between the death of an innocent person and the death of Christ: it reminds him of the Passion. Anamnesis.
Das Horenlied: In der ersten Tagesstund . . . Umb drei . . . Umb sechs . . . Zur neunden Stund . . . Zur Vesperzeit . . .	Brecht's preoccupation with time and with the Passion combinationally expressed through a Song of the Hours; the ninth hour's abandonment, cf. *Die Bibel*, outline commentary, p. 21; the sixth hour's *nackt und bloß*, cf. *Baal, Der Choral vom großen Baal*; the ninth hour's *Essig*, cf. *Mahagonny*, outline commentary p. 62; *Vesperzeit*, cf. Brecht's use of *Abend* in *Mahagonny*, outline commentary, p. 58.
Stehn Sie auch nicht herum wie Jesus am Ölberg, . . .	Proverb "Wie Ochs am Berg" altered to a mild blasphemy by inserting Jesus and the Mount of Olives manages to suggest the Agony in the Garden, and though distorted by Mutter Courage ("herumstehen!"), the allusion is psychologically justified since it unconsciously reflects his, her, and their, waiting to see what will become of Schweizerkas, and its use here reflects as well a dreadful cynicism as to the eventual outcome.

Table 4 *(continued)*

Die Bestechlichkeit ist bei die Menschen dasselbe wie beim lieben Gott die Barmherzigkeit.	free biblical-style creation by Brecht somewhat in the manner of Proverbs.
Zwei Landsknechte kommen mit einer Bahre, auf der unter einem Laken etwas liegt. Hebt ihn auf. Gebt ihn auf den Schindanger. Er hat keinen, der ihn kennt. (Feldwebel)	The abandonment, the not-being-acknowledged, the necessary denial of knowing the man, evokes the situation of the Death of Christ. Cf. the similar situation in Scene 12, as well as the ending of *Mahagonny*, in which the corpse of Paul Ackermann is also carried on a bier to accompanying chants from the Passion, outline commentary, pp. 62–63.
Sc. 8: [Die Menschheit muß hingehen durch Feuer und Schwert,] weil sie sündig ist von Kindesbeinen an. (Koch)	Paraphrase of Ps 51:7—Siehe, ich bin als Sünder geboren, und meine Mutter hat mich in Sünden empfangen. This emphasis may reflect a possible underlying Lutheran attitude on the nature of man.
Von Blei allein kann er [der Krieg] nicht leben.	Humorous adaptation of Mt 4:4 (Der Mensch lebt nicht vom Brot allein, . . .) to the situation of war.
Sc. 9: Frühwinter. Windstöße.	Cf. *Baal*, outline commentary, pp. 42–43.
Ihr saht den weisen Salomon. . . . Er verfluchte die Stunde seiner Geburt Und sah, daß alles eitel war.	Eccl (der Prediger Salomo) 1:2 *et passim*. Cursing specifically the day of one's birth, however, is from another part of the Wisdom literature which Brecht's memory seems to have conflated with Eccl, i.e., Job 3:3.
Hier seht ihr ordentliche Leut Haltend die zehn Gebot.	Ex 19–20. Cf. also commentary on *Mahagonny*, p. 60.
Sc. 10: Uns hat eine Ros ergetzet Im Garten mittenan	"Es ist ein' Ros' entsprungen/Aus einer Wurzel zart," seems to be suggested by the text and rhythm, and by Brecht's tendency to parody hymns.

Table 4 *(continued)*

	Here its winter tones emphasize the sadness of Mutter Courage's wandering. The carol is based on Is 11:10 as interpreted in Rom 15:12.
Sc. 11: Der Stein beginnt zu reden.	Lk 19:40, the beginning of the Lukan Passion account, the Palm Sunday entrance into the city [Wenn diese werden schweigen,]—so werden die Steine reden. Used here to presage the "miracle" of the dumb Kattrin's ability to "speak" and warn the city and thereby save it.
Es ist Nacht.	Possibly Jn 13:30, from the dramatic peak of the beginning of the Johannine Passion account, as Judas leaves the table of the Last Supper, John's Gospel makes the famous laconic comment: Und es war Nacht. Cf. outline commentary on *Mahagonny*, p. 58.
Gib ihm den Spieß in die Seit! (Fähnrich to second soldier concerning the young farmer)	Situational allusion to the Passion, Jn 19:34, der Kriegsknechte einer öffnete seine Seite mit einem Speer. This is also mentioned directly in the Vesperzeit stanza of the Horenlied in Scene 3 above: Ward Jesus in seine Seit/mit ein Speer gestochen.
Zwei Küh und ein Ochs. [7] Wenn du keine Vernunft annimmst, säbel ich das Vieh nieder. Nicht das Vieh! Die Bäuerin *weint*.	Insistence on the image of the ox suggests here an interesting similarity of image and argument to Isaiah's anger in Is 1:2–3 over sons not knowing parents (nicht kennen, as above with Schweizerkas) to Brecht's anger over peasants not quickly giving in when the young farmer is threatened, but immediately capitulating when their ox is; Mutter Courage's haste over spoiling bread, hesitation over threatened children. Ein Ochse kennt seinen Herrn, und ein Esel die Krippe seines Herrn; aber Israel kennt's nicht, und mein Volk versteht's nicht.

Table 4 *(continued)*

Und schönen Dank, Herr Hauptmann, daß Sie uns verschont haben, in Ewigkeit, Amen. (Bäuerin)	Prayer formula, bitterly showing the deification of the military. Cf. Scene 5 above—Setz dich zu meiner Rechten.
Bet, armes Tier, bet! Vater unser, der du bist im Himmel	Cf. commentary above, p. 74. The Lord's Prayer, Mt 6:99 ff., used here as a substitute for undertaking any real action to save the city because of the danger to self. Brecht's comment here on the use of prayer and liturgy to avoid deeds, is again surprisingly similar to Isaiah's anger against the same phenomenon in religious people. Und wenn ihr auch eure Hände ausbreitet [prayer position], verberge ich doch meine Augen vor euch; und wenn ihr auch viel betet, höre ich euch doch nicht; denn eure Hände sind voll Blut . . . Lernet Gutes tun, trachtet nach Recht, helft dem Unterdrückten, schaffet den Waisen Recht, führet der Witwen Sache! Is 1:10–17, and also 58:1–12.
Vater unser Vater unser, hör uns, denn nur du kannst helfen . . . der Feind ist vor den Mauern mit großer Macht. *Kattrin steht, verstört auf . . . hat sich . . . zum Wagen geschlichen, . . . und ist die Leiter hoch aufs Dach des Stalles geklettert.*	Both the biblical language in *die Bäuerin*'s prayer evokes the surrounded city of Judith, as well as Brecht's having Kattrin stand up to do something about it during the praying. Having her on the roof, so that the soldiers will be beneath her when they return to kill her, allows a visual suggestion of the Crucifixion scene, and will make the transformation of "Steig herab" to "Komm herunter" dramatically possible. Cf. below.
Gedenk der Kinder . . .	Litanaic prayer formulary combined with a "prudent" decision to inaction, made bitterly apparent to the audience through the obliviousness of *die Bäuerin*, and through the mention of forgiveness in the petition of the Our

Table 4 *(continued)*

	Father being prayed—as well as its violation at the time it is being prayed by the peasants and by the Catholic and Protestant armies.
Komm herunter (said by the first soldier, and by all the others in different ways)	Mt 27:40—Steig herab vom Kreuz! (said by the Pharisees and those surrounding the cross).
Sie trommelt aber weiter. . . . . *die letzten Schläge Kattrins werden von den Kanonen der Stadt abgelöst.*	Der Stein beginnt zu reden (above). This reminds one again of the theology of the Suffering Servant of Isaiah; Brecht has the sound of the gun that killed Kattrin be the means of the sound of her drum being taken up by the cannon of the city. This is the theology of Is 53:5—Aber er ist um unserer Sünde willen zerschlagen. Die Strafe liegt auf ihm auf daß wir Frieden hätten, und durch seine Wunden sind wir geheilt. This is also only a verse away from the "tat seinen Mund nicht auf, wie ein Lamm, das zur Schlachtbank geführt wird" in the same Isaiah text used above in connection with Christ's sufferings by Christian authors and in Catholic and Lutheran worship.
Kattrin, getroffen, schlägt noch einige Schläge und sinkt dann langsam zusammen. Sie hats geschafft. (erster Soldat)	Jn 19:30 [Da nun Jesus den Essig genommen hatte, sprach er] "Es ist vollbracht" und neigte das Haupt und verschied.
Sc. 12: *Vor dem Planwagen hockt Mutter Courage bei ihrer Tochter.*	visual suggestion of an unrealized Pietà. Cf. Mother Courage in Scene 1: Ich, schmerzensreiche Gebärerin.

From the commentary it is easily seen that both Scenes 3 and 11 are
combined with situational references to the Crucifixion of Christ so as
to create sympathy in the mind of the audience with the death of
Schweizerkas and Kattrin. Scripture is also used estrangingly in both
scenes, but not with reference to their deaths. In Scene 3, the references are at first so oblique as to be only subliminally effective, such
as "Ich bin unschuldig" and ". . . und hat das Maul nicht aufge-
macht" (cf. outline commentary, p. 75), but at the end they are almost tragically direct, "Er hat keinen, der ihn kennt" (commentary,
p. 76). However, in case the situation in the Thirty Years' War should
obscure his oblique insinuations of the death of Schweizerkas, as a
repetition of the death of the Innocent One, not only is Schweizerkas's honesty constantly extolled, but the *Feldprediger* himself interprets the death of Schweizerkas for the audience in a statement and a
Song of the Hours, a liturgical song, which becomes the center of the
scene. Referring to the bargaining over Schweizerkas, he says: "Solche Fäll sind in der Religionsgeschicht nicht unbekannt. Ich erinner
an die Passion von unserm Herrn und Heiland."[8] Perhaps the "Ich
erinner" is a clue to Brecht's theory of the repetition of the situations
of the Crucifixion in the Schweizerkases and Kattrins of his plays and
of the world. In the Christian tradition of worship and liturgy, *anamnesis* (remembering) has always been central. Remembering the Passion, Death (and Resurrection) is the center of the Holy Eucharist in
both Catholic and Lutheran worship, and it is the main function of
the priest or minister to lead this remembrance—and, appropriately
enough, it is the *Feldprediger* who leads the audience in remembering
it in this scene of the play. This is not to say that Brecht is writing a
Mass—but it is to say that he takes the remembering of the Passion,
which the churches use metaphysically (to attain access to God) and
changes that usage into an epistemological one, that is, a means of
recognizing and identifying what is happening whenever the weak,
innocent-good are made to die. This is, of course, exactly what Isaiah
did with the liturgical tradition of his day, and may account for
Brecht's predilection for the prophet who insisted on a new attitude
of mind toward the oppressed rather than the accurate celebration of
New Moons and Sabbaths; on refraining from overworking the slaves
rather than abstaining from various foods.

The Song of the Hours is a small masterpiece very much in the
medieval tradition of liturgy. Brecht has not only kept the traditional
form, but inserted his own emphasis within the framework. In the
second stanza the *innocence* of the accused is stated, together with
the irony of the accused being found innocent, and therefore, rather
than being released, he is sent to another judge so that some guilt

might be found in him. Brecht here has manipulated the evangelist's own ironical statement of Pilate's political "logic": "I find no guilt in this man, . . . *therefore* I will have him scourged" (Luke 23). Also in Brecht's hand the hours themselves bring out his horror that this extraordinary suffering can be imposed upon innocent people within the ordinary hours of ordinary days. He accomplishes this by the simple yet powerful device of twice omitting the expected word *Stunde.* Thus it is not the too-easily-mythologized "um die sechste Stunde," that is the time at which Christ is put upon the cross, but simply, and more horrifyingly, "Um sechs." The poet is trying to close the hermeneutic gap between the everyday crucifying of others, at which one feels little or no compunction, and the mythologized cruci- fying of Christ at which all feel a horror, but one that is at a convenient distance. After this "set–up," when Schweizerkas is actually brought in at the end of the scene, and his own people deny that they know him, this ancient denial of knowledge makes clear what Peter and his fellow human beings have brought upon themselves again.

In the larger scope of the play, this entire scene is a "set–up" for Scene 11, which is really the climax and synthesis of the play. The two scenes both employ the same form of the death of the Innocent being carried out by those who should know better, and who should do something to stop it, accompanied by direct and oblique situational references to the Passion and Death. Both scenes have a major liturgi- cal devotion as the center of the scene: the Song of the Hours in Scene 3, the Our Father in Scene 11.

Kattrin's death scene is presaged with the overtly biblical comment "Der Stein beginnt zu reden" (commentary, p. 77), and with the familiar Brechtian situation of "Es ist Nacht." The farmer and his wife are shown to value existence more than any morality when they remain silent as their son is threatened with a spear in the side (situa- tional allusion to the Passion), but react instantly to any threat of cold steel to the two cows and the ox upon which they are dependent for their livelihood. Brecht even has the farmer's wife thank the captain in such religious terms that make it clear that she is idolatrously putting him and military necessity in the place of God. Prayer is resorted to in the place of any action to save the city, and even Kattrin kneels down to pray for the city. The mention of the old people and, above all, the children in the city, the innocent, moves her with enough sympathy that she reacts by resolving to take action to warn the city. As the Our Father drones on, recited by those who are violating its every petition as they say it, she mounts the straw roof, so that she who is dumb may "call out" a warning to the city. The placing of her on the roof, the pulled-up ladder, and the constant insistence by those beneath her that she stop and come down, all serve to suggest that what happened in Scene 3 is happening again— "solche Fäll . . . sind in der Religionsgeschicht nicht unbekannt. . . ." And, just as no one was able to recognize who it was that was killed in Scene 3, so also here, the people devoutly praying the Lord's Prayer, do not recognize that their words: "Come down from there" have all been said before—by people who had to be forgiven because "they did not know what they were doing."

In this context we can understand the comment of the soldier who is standing under Kattrin's "cross": "Sie hats geschafft." One must say with the *Feldprediger*: "Ich erinner an die Passion. . . ." which is precisely what the author has arranged. "Es ist vollbracht."

Brecht could give no reason for risking one's existence, and *Mahagonny* pointed out that no one would do anything to save an ordinary person if it were going to cost anything. Here he has gone a long step beyond what he wrote before. Kattrin's drumming both warns and perhaps even saves the city, as did Judith's action; the disasters of *Die Bibel* and *Mahagonny* are averted. The children and the old people of the besieged city will not have to suffer, thanks to the self-sacrifice of one young woman. Brecht, who all along has been advocating action rather than inaction, has come to hope that self-sacrifice can pehaps ameliorate the sufferings of the weak at the hands of the strong, into whose hands they are always giving themselves. Once again his prefiguration of this rescue by self-sacrifice is from the New Testament, according to whose theology mankind was rescued by Christ's willingness to sacrifice himself to their machinations, and by his refusal to come down from the cross when they challenged him to do so. In this sense there is a great breakthrough in *Mutter Courage* towards an admittedly bleak form of optimism that does not exist in the earlier plays. Good is indeed shown to be impractical for the doer, even in the Song of the Virtues in *Mutter Courage* (commentary, p. 76), and Brecht is not distracted to belief in an afterlife in which virtue would be rewarded, but he does express the hope that it can perhaps after all accomplish something here. "Können jemand helfen." The weak can, even if at a great cost, help the weak.

This is, however, not the whole story. Scenes 3 and 11, heroic and empathetic though they may be, are placed within the context of Scenes 1 and 12. Kattrin's death and the successful warning of the city are not the final events of the play, the audience is not permitted to go home with Kattrin's heroism as the last thought in their minds. The curtain surprisingly comes up again, and there is the temporarily forgotten Mother Courage squatting next to her daughter, pathetically trying to sing a lullaby to her dead daughter. Now we return to the deep sadness of *Mahagonny*. "Können einem toten Mann nicht helfen." The canvas that covered the body at the end of Scene 3 to signify the absoluteness of the death of Schweizerkas, is brought forth again, this time to cover Kattrin.

The mother leaves her dead daughter to be buried, and departs to follow the war. And she is not singing a Song of the Hours or reciting the Our Father, but hoarsely reintones the pagan song of the continuation of war with which, in Scene 1, the play began. For a short time as she squatted on the ground next to the daughter whom she was unable to protect from the war, she provided an alienated visual image of the pietà, the Mother cradling the dead Crucified One, who had sacrificed himself for others. In Scene 1, she had already identified herself in these terms when she had referred to herself as "Ich, schmerzensreiche Gebärerin" (commentary, p. 72). But she has not learned, she does not see who she is as she squats next to her daughter, her great virtue is tenacity, not knowledge, and she moves on. And this new ending moves the audience as much as did the Kattrin ending.

Thus we come to the problem of the double ending of this play, the "Kattrin ending" and the "Mother Courage ending." Should the play be interpreted as optimistic, as a return to a nonideological humanism?—Kattrin did not save the city becaue it was Catholic or Protestant, communist or capitalist, but because the weak and innocent were in it: children. Or should it be interpreted pessimistically?—Mother Courage learns nothing and never will realize that she is *the* contributing cause of her children's death. She comes to realize as little about herself and war as the guinea pig does about biology. In biblical terms, in terms of one of the two Old Testament writers Brecht cites most, he is insisting in the Kattrin ending on the ultimate importance of man's essence of love and sympathy: "Brich dem Hungrigen dein Brot, und die, so im Elend sind, führe ins Haus; so du einen nackend siehest, so kleide ihn, und entzeuch dich nicht von deinem Fleisch" (Isaiah 58:5–7). And, he is extolling *doing* good over praying for it to happen: "Bringet nicht mehr Speisopfer so vergeblich. Das Rauchwerk ist mir ein Greuel; der Neumonden und Sabbathe da ihr zusammen kommet, und Mühe und Angst habt, derer mag ich nicht. . . . Waschet, reiniget euch, thut euer böses Wesen von meinen Augen, lasset ab vom Bösen; lernet Gutes thun, trachtet nach Recht, helfet dem Unterdrückten, schaffet dem Waisen Recht, und helfet der Witwen Sache" (Isaiah 1:13–17).

And is he not blaming nonrecognition of Israel's Parent as the cause of the continuation of the evil of war? It is interesting to note the diversity and yet the similarity of Isaiah's and Brecht's use of the ox-and-ass imagery in this context of the nonrecognition of family as the cause of war: "Höret, ihr Himmel, und Erde, nimm zu Ohren; denn der Herr redet: Ich habe Kinder auferzogen, und erhöhet, und sie sind von mir abgefallen. Ein Ochse kennet seinen Herrn, und ein Esel die Krippe seines Herrn; aber Israel kennet es nicht, und mein Volk vernimmt es nicht. . . . Euer Land ist verwüstet, eure Städte sind mit Feuer verbrannt; Fremde versehren eure Äcker vor euren Augen; . . . Übriggeblieben ist allein die Tochter Zion wie ein Häuslein im Weinberg, . . . wie eine *belagerte Stadt*" [emphasis mine] (Isaiah 1:2–3 & 7–8).

In the above passage, Isaiah is pleading with the people (who are suffering from war) in ironic anger, to be at least as human as animals. He uses the ox image to say that animals can recognize their masters and even the jackass knows his master's manger, but Israel does not seem to have the same capability of knowledge. One can compare this to the climactic scene in *Mutter Courage* in which Brecht also uses an ox image to protest that the peasants do not react when their own son's life is threatened, but react immediately when their ox and two cows are. Both Brecht and Isaiah are protesting against what they regard as improper priorities in human society, in which existence and economy are given first place over the family relationships of persons to persons—the relationship of the son to his parents, the relationship of children to their Parent. Isaiah protests against the hesitation of Israel to recognize its Father (and its brothers), with warfare as the result; Brecht protests against the hesitation of the peasants and Mother Courage to recognize their children, with the continuance of warfare and tragedy as the result. Furthermore, both Brecht and Isaiah realistically acknowledge the fate of anyone who says or does anything against this situation—he will be "led to the slaughter, and he will not open his mouth, like a lamb being led to the slaughter" (Isaiah 53:4).

The biblical approach to whether or not "to take up arms" against this sea of troubles is paradoxical, however, since the Wisdom tradition, especially in Brecht's other favorite author, Ecclesiastes, insists on the ineluctable transitoriness of all human existence, and thus on the ultimate futility and meaninglessness of all such humane, Isaian effort. "Ihr vergeht wie der Rauch und die Wärme" (commentary, p. 73). Death renders all things, even helping, useless:

Ihr saht den weisen Salomon
    . . .

Er verfluchte die Stunde seiner Geburt
Und sah, daß alles eitel war.
Kattrin sinkt dann langsam zusammen. (commentary, p. 79).

And, at the end, Mother Courage sits by the dead body of her Isaian daughter, who opened not her mouth, while she herself is drawn back into the cyclic, ever-returning new day of the war, fought by religious people. Vanity of Vanities. Thus the Mother Courage ending reflects the Wisdom tradition:

Der Feldzug ist noch nicht zu End!
Das Frühjahr kommt! Wach auf, du Christ!
Der Schnee schmilzt weg! Die Toten ruhn!
Und was noch nicht gestorben ist
Das macht sich auf die Socken nun. (GW, IV, 1438)

These lines, which go back to the beginning of the play, as we have seen make it clear that though Brecht advocates an Isaian approach to others, he is still ultimately more afraid of death than of anything else. It is not Kattrin who is resuscitated (the dead rest) but rather it is the war that returns, like *Baal*, in the spring. Whatever and whoever is "not yet" dead, had better get a move on. "'Not yet" indicates that Brecht holds both ends of the polarity of the Wisdom and the Prophetic traditions of his two most cited Old Testament authors. "Not yet" indicates both present life and the coming of death. It is both optimistic and pessimistic, and leaves the author free to see the crucifixions of his heroes and heroines in the mixed and paradoxical light of Isaiah and Ecclesiastes. This leaves little to no room for any New Testament resurrection of the good and innocent. Once one has sacrificed one's existence for the sake of one's human essence (love), it is indeed gone. The ultimate framework for the life and death of Kattrin is the living death of her mother. As in *Baal*, the tree is indeed great, but the space between the trees is greater. Or at least so it appears. Religious nihilism.

But the city is saved. Some others will be able to live a little longer, and if there is an "Our Father," perhaps it is from him that one will have to ask why the fate of the good person was so cruel on earth. And why it is that, through the loss of the sympathetic, weak individual, the strong city can be saved.

Brecht explores the problem of the fate of Kattrin-like characters in two subsequent plays, *Der gute Mensch von Sezuan* and *Der kaukasische Kreidekreis*, but does not return again to the full depth of tragedy that is present in *Mutter Courage und ihre Kinder*. I agree with Walter Sokel's controversial opinion, which, on a purely classical literary basis, classifies *Mutter Courage* as Brecht's closest approach to Greek tragedy.[9] The epistemological tragedy he finds in the conflict between fate and Mother Courage's unwitting role in the deaths of her children, is more than substantiated by what I have found of Brecht's use of the Bible. Brecht reinforces the twin nemeses of war and death through the use of Ecclesiastes; fear, and especially pity, are aroused through his use of the Crucifixion in connection with the deaths of two of the children; the hamartia of the heroine, the presumption that she can make a living off the war and haggle long enough to save her children, is exposed and condemned through his use of Isaiah and the Our Father.

Der gute Mensch von Sezuan is not a death tragedy, and thus the Passion and Death pattern that we have found so far is not to be found there. Biblical material, however, there certainly is, especially in view of the fact that Brecht is exploring the problem of having to be both good and evil. Thus Shen Te and Shui Ta, gentle as doves and wise as serpents, in order to survive in the world of relatives and property. The biblical material that lies at the base of the play is Genesis 18:20–19:29, the Abraham and Lot story, and the search for just one good man in the city of Sodom. The Three Visitors to Abraham's tent are asked the question that was put just above—why is the fate of the good person so cruel on earth? The old theological question of Job is raised again in the simplest and most difficult terms: if creation has been made by God, who is all-good, why is it that a good man is forced by circumstances to compromise with evil in order to survive there? At the end of the play the Three go off, encouraging Shen Te/Shui Ta, but bumblingly unable to give any answer.

In *Der kaukasische Kreidekreis* we find once again the situation of the city besieged, though this time it is at the beginning of the play and not at the end. Like *Der gute Mensch von Sezuan*, this play is quite overtly a parable and the opposite of a tragedy. It was written about six years after the completion of *Mutter Courage*, and is something of a "comedy" to that tragedy, no doubt affected by the coming of the end of World War II. Death and its horrors do not play a determining role and the Crucifixion pattern is thereby necessarily absent, even though the basic matter is still biblical, being based on I Kings 3:13–28, Solomon's decision between the two mothers on who was the mother of the child. Brecht modifies the biblical matter by transposing it onto a Russian landscape, by using it as a paradigm for the problem of ownership, and by changing the nature of Solomon to a very Brechtian judge, who drinks and lives loosely and dispenses authentic justice through bribery and kindness, but at the climax it is still Solomon's Decision that is being hermeneutically explored, and the self-sacrifice of the good person has, once again, actually helped someone.

In many respects, the *Kreidekreis* represents a resolution of the problem with which we began in *Die Bibel*, where human uprightness was the cause of so much suffering and the fall of the city, and where human weakness, in the form of the Father, had to be ashamed of itself. In the magic, almost liturgical world of the *Kreidekreis* parable (which is for Brecht a never-never land, one suspects, since death is not present to have the last say there) the opposite world to that of *Die Bibel* is projected. Human weakness in the form of Azdak (where there is again parallelism to the Passion) and human kindness in the form of Grusche bring about a temporary era of justice and peace. The severity of the grandfather and the idealism (later to become ideology) of the brother, are replaced by the gentle vices of Azdak; the hesitation of the daughter to risk herself for the sake of her town is replaced by Grusche's sympathy for the child; the gentle tolerant weakness of the father triumphs, even if only for a brief mythic time, in the humane kingdom of Azdak. The temptation to do good ceases to be so dangerous. "Kattrin" is rewarded with a child, and Grusche says in her last statement, in this last of Brecht's great plays, that which has always been missing from his use of the Passion and Death, ". . . an diesem Ostertag."

The siege is, for the moment at least, lifted.

VI

Conclusions

It has been the aim of this study to identify and explicate the way in which Bertolt Brecht uses the Bible in his plays in which death plays a major role and, if possible, to specify the "noch mehr" of Hans Mayer—referred to in the Introduction.

It is my first conclusion that Brecht is no outsider to the Bible. He is not simply and solely "using" it as convenient and effective propaganda to further Marxist aims. Garner's conclusions along these lines seem to me to be the result of a too ideologically oriented study with insufficient attention to the actual uses of the Bible within the dramas.[1] Garner's concluding statement in his dissertation that Brecht denigrates liturgical imagery as a means of building up Marxist, secular theatre, and that parody of the Bible and of Christianity is his major didactic and propagandistic vehicle, I find to be a great oversimplification. That Brecht parodies biblical language: yes; that he parodies its moral theology of kindness and love: yes and no; that he parodies Ecclesiastes, Job, Isaiah, and the Passion and Death accounts of Matthew and John: absolutely not. I think it is further possible to state that the Passion accounts, as well as biblical Wisdom and Prophetic literature, were employed not so much as aids to propaganda, but both when he was younger (*Die Bibel*) and older (*Mutter Courage*) very much for their own sakes. This is due to Brecht's eudaemonistic acceptance of the profound struggle with the realities of human weakness and individual death that is to be found in Ecclesiastes, Isaiah, and the Passion—a profound struggle shared with these Books by Brecht's mind and soul as a dramatist both prior to adherence to institutional communism, during his time of growing acceptance of it (as exemplified in *Mahagonny*), and thereafter.

Brecht's overriding concern both with the question of the worthwhileness of being good, and of the death by crucifixion of those who attempt to be good, makes him immediately a person capable of profound empathy with those Books that make these issues their deepest concern and those whose imagery and argument he in turn used in his plays. No ideology, Marxist or otherwise, makes of these twin concerns, goodness and death, the central concern that religion in general and the Bible in particular, make of them. Hence Brecht's lifelong attachment to the Bible, and especially to those parts of the Bible that make them their central issue.[2] Brecht's citations and situational allusions clearly link those writings with his overriding concerns: Ecclesiastes with the problem of death, Isaiah with social goodness, Matthew with the death of the Good Person.

It is my second conclusion that the Passion of Christ is for Brecht the archetypal synthesis of these two concerns that so occupied him, and it is for this reason that we find the Crucifixion pattern in all four plays, from "Mein Gott, mein Gott, warum hast du mich verlassen?" which begins the fifteen-year old's *Die Bibel*, to "Sie hat's geschafft," which concludes the Kattrin episode of the forty-year old's *Mutter Courage*.

Thirdly, Brecht's *Verfremdung* (situational estrangement) in his use of the Passion and Death in all four works is not an attempt at alienation—neither of the subject matter nor of the audience—but rather an attempt to gain audience sympathy for the morally weak, the poor, and the helpless, and to increase audience alienation from the morally righteous, the wealthy, and the powerful. It is an attempt to expose the tragedy of the mortal's *condition humaine* as Brecht saw it exposed in the archetype thereof with which he and the audience had the greatest ability to identify: the Crucifixion of Christ. This identification is not merely aesthetic, but rather it is an hermeneutic one made by the poet in order to close the gap of genuine alienation between the audience's daily nonrecognition and acceptance of the everyday crucifixions of the poor and helpless as seen in Brecht's newspapers, and their active recognition and rejection of the evil of the classical Crucifixion of Christ. Brecht's lifelong dramatic empathy with the Crucifixion and his horror at the repetition of the crucifixion are the roots of the "noch mehr." His use of the Bible is here identifying rather than distancing, and epistemological rather than metaphysical. This modifies, but does not contradict, the observations made by previous researchers on Brecht's constant satirizing of other parts of the Bible and of Christianity.

Fourth. The form of the use of the Passion and Death is parallel to liturgical *anamnesis* through suggestion, in the unique form of *situational allusion*. That is to say, the occurrence of present events on the stage reminds one of the past event, not so clearly that all the lines of Pilate, say, are repeated in the drama by a precisely identifiable "Pilate figure," or Peter's lines by a precise "Peter figure," etc., as in standard allusions in a classical "Aristotelian" *drama*. Rather, the ancient situation is more obliquely recreated through the use of a more subtly audience-involving *epic* technique, as in the liturgy of the Church.

The allusions to the Agony in the Garden, for example, can be made as much by Mother Courage as by Schweizerkas himself, as long as the situation on the stage is the ancient situation of agonized waiting prior to death. Christ's "It has been accomplished" can be put into the mouth of a soldier, as long as Kattrin has died up above them on the roof. The essence of the technique seems to be to provide for a recurrence of the ancient situation, in such a way that the other characters "do not know what they are doing" and the audience feels moved because it senses the ancient parallel, without being totally aware of it.

Fifth. There is a pattern in those parts of the Passion and Death to which Brecht constantly refers, which may be useful for psychological studies of his themes. Of all the multiple aspects of the Crucifixion that were at his disposal, in the four plays studied, Brecht tends to refer consistently to: a) the suffering of personal abandonment rather than the physical sufferings of the Passion; b) Peter's betrayal, "I do not know him" (the betrayal of a friend), rather than the Judas betrayal (for money) which, from the conventional anticapitalist image of Brecht, one might have been led to expect;[3] c) time: the times of the day and night from Matthew's Passion are used to unify the cosmic and the everyday dimension of finality of the Passion and Death, this finality receiving rather more emphasis than the authority figures causing the Crucifixion and Death. This tends to corroborate Ralph Ley's findings on the effects of Brecht's scientific view of space-time as causing in him a eudaemonistically tragic feeling of "cosmic futility."[4]

Sixth. I have come to the conclusion that the "conventional wisdom" on Brecht's atheism must be modified. The question of the mystery of God is a constant presence in Brecht's works. The God whose existence he denies is the God of explanations, the God who is supposedly behind conventional moral conduct and against progress, the God of Job's friends. There is indeed no God for the people and the founders of Mahagonny—but is there a God to receive the dying weak, a God of the innocent, the God of the dying Baal, Paul Ackermann, Kattrin, and Jesus Christ? That is the question from which he can never seem to separate himself even though he is never able to give a definitive "yes" answer to it. Brecht himself once remarked in East Berlin about two years before his death, in reference to some of the very negative verses he had written as a young man in the *Hauspostille*: "Der den großen Sprung machen will, muß einige Schritte zurückgehen."[5] A man concerned all his life with stepping back, is aware of the jump, even if he cannot bring himself to run forward to make the leap.

This study has been restricted to Brecht's use of the Bible, yet it tends, indirectly perhaps, to raise the question of the persistently negative role of the church in Brecht's drama. While I do not intend in any way to give a complete answer to this question, I would like to suggest a direction for future research.

Brecht's highly selective attitude toward the different books of the Bible may well be paralleled by an analogous attitude toward the sociopolitical structure of Christianity. The high authority figures in the church, and the church as a behavior-controlling force, are clearly rejected. Trinity-Moses in *Mahagonny*, the grandfather (by analogy) in *Die Bibel*, popes-and-generals in *Mutter Courage*, all use their religious power and authority to create tragically enticing situations—war, the city—where the common man is doomed. Lower-level figures in the sociopolitical structure of the church, however, are treated with a more mixed touch of sympathy and rejection. The country pastor in *Baal* who protects his flock from their own cupidity and then pays for Baal's drinks at the bar, is treated with an easy, almost friendly, familiarity. The military chaplain in *Mutter Courage* is shown to be, like her, unaware of his complicity in prolonging the tragedy of war: he is, on the one hand, proud of his ability by preaching to fire up the soldiers for battle, but then he exhausts himself pulling the dying out from under the ruins of war and bandaging their wounds. And it all reminds him of the Passion.

Perhaps the play that would give the best stage presentation for a study of this attitude toward the church would be the *Leben des Galilei*, since the whole ladder of church authority figures is present. One might contrast Brecht's somewhat dialectical rejection of the powerful cardinals with his apparent acceptance of Father Clavius and the little monk. The moment of synthesis comes in the capitulation of the new pope to his new authoritarian role,[6] as he gives in to the Inquisitor on the Galilei question. As mere priest and mathematician, Berberini (perhaps one could say, the church) is solicitous both for scientific truth and for Galilei. As his papal vesting progresses, however, it visibly raises him up the ladder of church authority roles, and progressively weakens his humane resolve until, when fully robed in vestments and tiara, as pope, his (the church's?) humanity is so weakened that he gives in to the organizational needs presented by the Cardinal Inquisitor. He surrenders his own personal attitude, which had been that of Clavius and the little monk, and accedes to that of the "organization men," the cardinals.

Seventh. Brecht finds both in Isaiah and in the "Social Gospel" of Matthew and Luke a gospel of praising the weak and defenseless over the strong. Brecht might prefer to change "Blessed are the peace-makers" to "Crucified are the peacemakers," but that is a change which each of the four Evangelists would acknowledge as also veri-fied in the latter part of each of their Gospels! Brecht is able to find in the Passion narrative a value placed on fundamental human frailty to oppose the "strength" of the moral demands made in the earlier parts of the same Gospels, and he is able to find in Isaiah both a similar concern for the poor and the weak, and a similar attitude toward the problem of the origin of social evil: they "do not know," they "do not realize," what they are doing.

Brecht finds in Ecclesiastes and the Wisdom literature a religious attitude of mind that is similar to his own views on the ultimate finality of death as rendering all things useless and "a striving for the wind."

Furthermore, Brecht cannot in consequence evade the dilemma of the *futility* versus the usefulness of helping. He cannot decide whether man is ultimately a mortal or a moral being, or, biblically speaking, whether Ecclesiastes or Isaiah is more ultimately correct about the nature of man. Unable to avoid the dilemma, he transforms it into a dialectic of doubt about the final value of a self-sacrificing good deed for others—especially the deaths of Kattrin, Paul, and Christ himself. This is most clearly reflected in the structure and the double ending of *Mutter Courage*.

Eighth. Brecht accepts the distinction between existence and es-sence. "Erst kommt das Fressen, dann kommt die Moral," is the rule in the city of man. This point of view, while seemingly areligious if religion is taken primarily as morality, is actually deeply in accord with both medieval Thomistic thought, and with the Wisdom litera-ture of the Bible, where the Divine is thought of in terms of existence rather than in terms of morality. This concurrence enables Brecht to place sympathy with the death of Baal above agreement or disagree-ment with the morality of his actions; it enables Brecht to depict Jenny as loving Paul but not sacrificing her existence (money) for him; it enables him to depict Mother Courage torn between her double es-sence as mother and business-woman as she attempts to deal with the threat to her existence and to the existence of her children from the war; it enables him to prefer the father to the grandfather or the brother.

Brecht's biologically serious acceptance of death enables him to take the Crucifixion itself as something the believing Christian can-not: a final tragedy. A poet might be tempted to describe him as a kind of Old-Testament Ecclesiastes or Isaiah standing outside the city wall, looking in disbelief at the Corpse on the cross of Calvary, as it is getting dark, toward evening, and mumbling over and over again, "Vanity of vanities . . . love thy neighbor . . . vanity of vanities. . . ."

But Baal is listening to the rain: "Ich horche noch auf den Regen, sagte er" (GW, I, 67).

Notes

Chapter 1

1. Brecht had been asked the question of what was "der stärkste Eindruck" on his writing. The now famous answer was printed in the Berlin ladies' magazine *Die Dame* of 1 October 1928. Cf. Martin Esslin, *Brecht: The Man and His Work* (New York: Doubleday, Anchor Books, 1961), p. 106.

2. Siegfried Mews concludes his extensive review essay devoted to studies of Brecht and world literature with the following remark: "It is an indication of the areas still to be explored that so far, despite repeated references to the prominence of Biblical influences in Brecht's work, no comprehensive study is available on the subject." Siegfried Mews, "Bertolt Brecht and World Literature," *Papers on Language and Literature*, 13 (1977), 108.

3. Martin Esslin's essay provides a typical example: "Brecht's language also has a firm basis in the chief source of modern standard German. . . . And in fact the vigorous, outspoken language of Luther's Bible pervades the writings of the atheist and blasphemer Brecht. He made masterly use of biblical construction: the juxtaposition of contrasted half-sentence, parallelisms, repetition, and inversion. Equally marked throughout Brecht's life was the influence of the street ballad. . . . Esslin, ibid.

4. Recent study indicates that the latter view is the more probable. W. Frisch and K. W. Obermeier cite the following on Brecht's father in *Brecht in Augsburg: Erinnerungen, Texte, Fotos; eine Dokumentation* (Frankfurt/M: Suhrkamp, 1976), p. 22: "Er war ein nüchterner, liberal eingestellter Mann. Kam das Gespräch einmal auf religiöse Fragen, dann sei er ernst geworden und habe gesagt: 'Das kann jeder halten, wie er's will.' "

5. Cf. Reinhold Grimm, "Brecht's Beginnings" in *Brecht*, ed. Erika Munk (New York: Bantam, 1972), p. 26 (first published in *The Drama Review*, 12, [Fall, 1967]).

6. Ronald Gray did not know of the existence of *Die Bibel* at the time of his book, but even without this evidence, he attaches the same importance to Brecht's mixed religious background as does the present author. Cf. Ronald Gray, *Bertolt Brecht* (New York: Grove, 1961), pp. 2–3.

7. Marianne Kesting, *Bertolt Brecht in Selbstzeugnissen und Bilddokumenten* (Hamburg: Rowohlt, 1959), pp. 12–13.

8. Hans Mayer, *Bertolt Brecht und die Tradition* (Pfullingen: Neske, 1961), p. 50.

9. Bertolt Brecht, *Gesammelte Werke in 20 Bänden* (Frankfurt/M: Suhrkamp, 1967), I, 249. Hereafter abbreviated as GW followed by volume (Roman numeral) and page (Arabic numeral).

10. Paul Konrad Kurz, *Über moderne Literatur* (Frankfurt/M: Josef Knecht, 1969), Vol. II, p. 54. Trans. Sr. Mary Frances McCarthy as *On Modern German Literature* (University, Alabama: University of Alabama Press, 1971).

11. Ibid., p. 84.

12. Reinhold Grimm, *Bertolt Brecht: Die Struktur seines Werkes* (Nürnberg: Hans Carl, 1962), pp. 44–45.

13. Ibid.

14. Grimm, *Brecht: Die Struktur seines Werkes*, p. 45.

15. Grimm later modified his opinion on Brecht's use of the Bible and referred, much more accurately I believe, to Brecht's "lebenslange und höchst komplexe Abhängigkeit von der Bibel" in Reinhold Grimm, *Bertolt Brecht und die Weltliteratur* (Nürnberg: Hans Carl, 1961), p. 5.

16. Barbara Allen Woods, "A Man of Two Minds," *The German Quarterly*, 42 (1969), 46.

17. Thomas O. Brandt, "Brecht und die Bibel" *PMLA*, 79 (1964), 176.

18. Gary Neil Garner, "Bertolt Brecht's Use of the Bible and Christianity in Representative Dramatic Works." Diss., Louisiana State University, 1969. Available from University Microfilms, Ann Arbor, Michigan.

19. Hans Pabst, *Brecht und die Religion* (Graz: Styria, 1977).

20. Henry Hatfield, *Modern German Literature, The Major Figures in Context* (London: Edward Arnold, 1966), p. 136.

21. Mayer, *Brecht und die Tradition*, p. 50.

22. Ibid., pp. 51–52.

23. Ibid.

24. Ibid.

25. In April 1977, the author received a letter from the *Brecht-Archiv* in Berlin, informing him that, in response to his request that a search be made for a possible copy of the Bible in Brecht's library, a small, well-marked, pocket edition had been found. On the flyleaf was written: *bertolt brecht 1926*, in his own handwriting. The present author's analysis of the marked scriptural passages, which substantially corroborate the present work, can be found in: "Brecht's Pocket Bible," *The German Quarterly*, 50 (1977), 474–84.

Chapter 2

1. What is known about this very early work is given succinctly in the new Suhrkamp edition of Brecht's works: "Das 'Drama in einem Akt' ist wahrscheinlich das erste abgeschlossene Stück Brechts. Er schrieb es mit 15 Jahren als Schüler des Realgymnasiums in Augsburg und veröffentlichte es im Januar 1914 unter dem Namen Bertold Eugen im sechsten hektografierten Heftchen der Schülerzeitschrift 'Die Ernte,' für die er viele Beiträge verfaßte" (GW, VII, *Anmerkungen*, 5).

2. Reinhold Grimm has noted that the kernel of plays written at much later dates can be found in *Die Bibel*.

In Brecht's earliest play the seeds of his central themes are clearly apparent throughout. Who does not recall these affecting verses in *The Good Women of Setzuan* in which the destruction by fire which *Die Bibel* embodies returns so inescapably? Shen Te refers to the story of Sodom and Gomorrah, and thus also to the Bible.

If in a city an injustice is done, there must be a protest—
And where these is no protest, it would be better that the city be destroyed
By fire, before night falls.

Or we might pursue the motive of sacrifice for the community, which returns with such tragic remorselessness in Brecht's didactic play *Die Maßnahme*—where the reference to the Bible cannot be ignored, the half consecrated, half blasphemous scene in which the young comrade "in the interest of Communism" is shot to death, and thrown into a lime pit. And the figure of the girl! This pallid, almost faceless creature is the mother of all touching maiden figures in Brecht's work, from Joan in the slaughterhouse of Chicago to dumb Kattrin in the Thirty Years' War. Further: Brecht, in 1914, had seen the new man. Even his duality, the duality of Galileo, is prefigured in *Die Bibel*. The grandfather says specifically: "We are not willing to recant . . . we will go to our destruction, if need be—for our faith."

For not only would the girl have to be sacrificed, but all the inhabitants would have to abjure their faith for the city to be spared."

The preceding is from Grimm's article "Brecht's Beginnings" in *Brecht*, ed. Erika Munk (New York: Bantam, 1972), pp. 28–29.

3. I am very much in agreement with the interpretation of *Verfremdung* given by Ernst Bloch, who regards it as primarily a method of attaining artistic contemplative distance from the action or event or character being portrayed in order to arrive at insight concerning it. Cf. Ernst Bloch, "*Entfremdung, Verfremdung*: Alienation, Estrangement," in *Brecht*, ed. E. Munk, pp. 3–11.

4. Book 5, Ch. V; trans. Constance Garnett (New York: Modern Library, 1950), pp. 255–74.

5. "Margarete mit einer Lampe. 'Es ist so schwül, so dumpfig hie . . . Ich wollt', die Mutter käm' nach Haus.' " From the *Abend* scene in *Faust*—in the Hamburger Ausgabe (Hamburg: Wegner, 1965), III, 88 (Verses 2753–56).

6. Brecht may also have reacted to the Hebbel version of the Judith story as well as to the original version. Seven years later (in 1921) he made the following observation on Hebbel's *Judith*: "Es ist eines der schwächsten und albernsten Stücke unseres klassischen deutschen Repertoires. Aber das gleiche Schwein, das die Lulu [Wedekind's heroine] für eine Beschimpfung der Frau hält, schwärmt für die Judith" (GW, XV, 37). For a discussion of the Brecht-Hebbel question, see Dieter Schmidt, *Baal und der junge Brecht: Eine textkritische Untersuchung zur Entwicklung des Frühwerks* (Stuttgart: Metzler, 1966), pp. 19–24.

Chapter 3

1. Martin Esslin, *Brecht: The Man and His Work* (Garden City, N.Y.: Doubleday & Co., Inc., Anchor Books, 1961), p. 7.

2. *Baal und der junge Brecht: Eine textkritische Untersuchung zur Entwicklung des Frühwerks* (Stuttgart: Metzler, 1966), pp. 30–32.

3. Ibid., p. 32.

4. "Im Sommersemester 1918 hält Brecht im theaterwissenschaftlichen Seminar Artur Kutschers in München ein Referat über Hanns Johsts Roman *Der Anfang*. In seine scharfe Kritik bezieht er auch das übrige Werk des Schriftstellers ein und erklärt, daß er zu dessen idealistischem Drama *Der Einsame* ein Gegenstück: *Baal*, schreiben werde." Dieter Schmidt, *Bertolt Brecht. Baal. Drei Fassungen* (Frankfurt/M: Suhrkamp, 1966), p. 190.

5. Hanns Johst, *Der Einsame: Ein Menschenuntergang* (Munich: Albert Langen, 1925 [1st Edition, 1917]), p. 25.

6. Ibid., pp. 26–27.

7. All page references are to the 1925 Langen edition cited above.

8. Easy access to the text was available in any reference work, e.g., *Kirchliches Handlexikon*, ed. Michael Buchberger (Freiburg i. Br.: Herdersche Verlagshandlung, 1907), (article on *Baal*, p. 439) as well as through the Bible itself.

9. Marianne Kesting, *Bertolt Brecht in Selbstzeugnissen und Bilddokumenten* (Hamburg: Rowohlt, 1959), p. 16.

10. Cf. *Baal* article in the *Encyclopaedia Judaica* (Jerusalem: Keter/Macmillan, 1972), Vol. 4, pp. 9–10.

11. John L. McKenzie, S.J., *Dictionary of the Bible* (Milwaukee: Bruce, 1965), p. 72.

12. Cf. D.P. Meyer-Lenz's article "Brecht und der Pflaumenbaum," in *Neue Deutsche Hefte*, 18, No. 1 (1971), pp. 40–48.

13. This is the mythic origin of the cultic practice condemned in Ez 8:13–14, "und siehe, daselbst saßen Weiber, die weinen über den Thamus," of weeping over the death of Baal-Tammuz (god-summer).

14. *Encyclopaedia Judaica*, as cited above, Vol. 4, pp. 10–11.

15. GW, I, 26. In further citations from *Baal*, in this chapter, the page will be indicated in parentheses at the end of the quotation.

16. Brecht claimed later that this last scene (22) was in his original version as he first wrote it, and asked that it be retained in the definitive version. Cf. GW, I, *Anmerkungen*, p. 3. He thus insisted on an ending that strongly asserted that beyond death the cycle of life would continue to go on and that rains will come again in the spring.

17. *Bertolt Brecht. Baal. Drei Fassungen*, ed. Dieter Schmidt (Frankfurt/M: Suhrkamp, 1966), p. 75.

18. I find nothing to support Garner's contention that Solomon's Song of Songs is the main biblical influence on/or parallel to Brecht's *Baal*. Cf. Gary Neil Garner, "Bertolt Brecht's Use of the Bible and Christianity in Representative Dramatic Works" (Diss., Louisiana State University, 1969), pp. 52 ff.

19. Cf. early fragment of an oratory in Werner Frisch and K. W. Obermeier, *Brecht in Augsburg: Erinnerungen, Texte, Fotos; eine Dokumentation* (Frankfurt/M: Suhrkamp, 1976), p. 278.

20. McKenzie, *Dictionary of the Bible*, pp. 72–78.

Chapter 4

1. Brecht later changed the name of the play so as to avoid mentioning Lindbergh. He gave his reasons in a letter in 1950 to the *Süddeutscher Rundfunk*:

Lindbergh hat bekanntlich zu den Nazis enge Beziehungen unterhalten; sein damaliger enthusiastischer Bericht über die Unbesieglichkeit der Nazi-Luftwaffe hat in einer Reihe von Ländern lähmend gewirkt. Auch hat L. in den USA als Faschist eine dunkle Rolle gespielt. In meinem Hörspiel muß daher der Titel in *Der Ozeanflug* umgeändert werden, man muß den Prolog sprechen und den Namen Lindbergh ausmerzen.

Or, as he put it in his other type of language in the *Prolog*: "Der sich zurechtfand über weglosen Wassern/Verlor sich im Sumpf unserer Städte. Sturm und Eis/Besiegte ihn nicht, aber der Mitmensch/Besiegte ihn" (GW, II, *Anmerkungen*, 1–3).

2. The German version reads: "Auch weiß der Mensch seine Zeit nicht, sondern wie die Fische gefangen werden mit dem verderblichen Netz und wie die Vögel mit dem Garn gefangen werden, so werden auch die Menschen verstrickt zur bösen Zeit, wenn sie plötzlich über sie fällt."

3. Jn 4:14—see also the outline commentary, pp. 00–00.

4. Gunter Sehm finds the entire structure of the play to be based on the structure of the Bible. In a well drawn parallel he finds the play's structure to be based on Exodus, the Old and New Law, the Passion and Death. Cf. his "Moses, Christus und Paul Ackermann: Brechts *Aufstieg und Fall der Stadt Mahagonny*" in the *Brecht-Jahrbuch 1976* (Frankfurt/M: Suhrkamp, 1976), pp. 85–96.

5. Cf. Siegfried Mews, "Biblical Themes and Motifs in Brecht's *Herr Puntila und sein Knecht Matti*," *The University of Dayton Review*, 13 (Spring 1979), 53–63.

6. Willett has noted the frequency of these "St. Peter-like episodes." Cf. John Willett, *The Theatre of Bertolt Brecht* (New York: New Directions, 1968), p. 83.

7. On a recent visit to Brecht's house on the Chausseestraße in East Berlin, I was surprised to see the two worn, wooden statues he had placed above the mantelpiece on the fireplace wall: Mary and John from an old crucifixion scene.

Chapter 5

1. He apparently left so quickly on the morning after the *Reichstag* fire, that he didn't even return to his apartment. Cf. Klaus Völker, *Brecht: A Biography* (New York: Seabury Press, 1978), pp. 168 ff.

2. By 1936, the rearmament of Germany, the occupation of the Rhineland, and the outbreak of the Spanish Civil War had come. The *Anschluß* in 1938 and Nazi control of Czechoslovakia in 1939, together with the increasing impetus toward war with Poland, must have persuaded Brecht that it was time to move on. In April of 1939 he fled to Sweden with his wife and two children. In 1940 he was in Finland, heading for Vladivostok and America. *Mutter Courage* was written under these conditions of fear and of the need to keep moving on for survival's sake, a condition reflected in the wariness and the insecurity of the constantly moving *Marketenderin*, Anna Fierling. Cf. Frederic Ewen, *Bertolt Brecht: His Life, His Art, His Times* (New York: Citadel, 1967), pp. 292–94.

3. From the excellent introductory chapter in Ralph Manheim and John Willett's *Bertolt Brecht, Collected Plays* (New York: Random House, Vintage, 1972), V, viii.

4. Ibid., pp. vii–ix.

5. Ibid., p. ix. In one of these poems the reaction of Brecht the moralist to the death of Serge Tretiakov is evident even in the title, *Ist das Volk unfehlbar?*

6. (GW, IV, 1470–71) *Faber* is the Latin (Vulgate) New Testament's term for translating the famous question on Jesus's identity in Mt 13:55: *Nonne hic est fabri filius?* (Is this not the carpenter's son?), and is the standard Latin term used whenever reference is made to the Carpenter, or *Zimmermann*, of Nazareth. The cadence in the passage, however, is that of his youthful Absalom, Absalom, my son Absalom.

7. Herbert Knust has noted the importance of Brecht's ox-imagery and describes it as follows: "Die Welt ist ein blutiges Schlachthaus: Vieh, Packherren, Arbeiten und sogar der liebe Gott werden—vereint durch das zentrale Bild des brüllenden abschlachtbaren Ochsen (dem man das Maul nicht verbinden soll)—zur konsumierenden und konsumierbaren Ware gestempelt." Cf. his article "Brechts Dialektik vom Fressen und von der Moral" in *Brecht Heute-Brecht Today*, Vol. 3, ed. Gisela Bahr et al. (Frankfurt/M: Athenäum, 1973), p. 237.

8. (GW, IV, 1384). Cf. commentary, p. 000.

9. "Brecht's plays of split characters are akin to Greek tragedies insofar as they show an external necessity acting in and by the individual as a destructive barrier to his desire. The threat of starvation forces Mother Courage to support a war which devours her children one by one . . . one pattern of Greek tragedy prevails: Necessity, the condition of human existence, defeats the aspirations, nobility and greatness of man. The split nature of his (Brecht's) protagonists serves Brecht as his device for presenting this tragic pattern. . . . There is . . . neither a development toward a tragic event, as in *Macbeth*, nor a development toward a tragic revelation, as in *Oedipus*. Instead Brecht demonstrates a tragic situation [which, I maintain, is the crucifixion situation]; he holds it up to our inspection. Of all Brecht's plays *Mother Courage*, by its structure, comes closest to the traditional pattern of European tragedy." Walter H. Sokel, "Brecht's Split Characters and His Sense of the Tragic," in *Brecht: A Collection of Critical Essays*, ed. Peter Demetz (Englewood Cliffs, N.J.: Prentice-Hall, 1962), pp. 133–35.

Chapter 6

1. Gary Neil Garner, "Bertolt Brecht's Use of the Bible and Christianity in Representative Dramatic Works" (Diss., Louisiana State University, 1969), pp. 191–93.

2. It is interesting to recall Brecht's retort to a friend who wished to engage him in a religious discussion even when he was on his way to East Berlin: "Geben Sie acht, wenn Sie mit mir über Glaubensfragen diskutieren, mein Lieber. Ich bin der letzte römischkatholische Kopf!" in Ernst Ginsberg, *Abschied, Erinnerungen, Theateraufsätze, Gedichte* (Zurich: Arche, 1965), p. 144.

3. The Judas betrayal, however, is also used in other plays, for example, *Leben Eduards des Zweiten von England*. Cf. p. 5.

4. Cf. Ralph Ley's article, "Brecht: Science and Cosmic Futility," *The Germanic Review*, 40 (1965), 205–24.

5. Quoted by Thomas O. Brandt, "Brecht und die Bibel," *PMLA*, 79 (1964), 172, n.

6. Brecht's exposition of the problems of the individual in an authoritarian role is remarkably confirmed in Milgram's now classic experiment. Stanley Milgram, *Obedience to Authority: An Experimental View* (New York: Harper and Row, 1974), esp. pp. 137–64.

Selected Bibliography

I. PRIMARY SOURCES

Brecht, Bertolt. *Gesammelte Werke in 20 Bänden*. Frankfurt/M: Suhrkamp, 1967.
———. *Collected Plays*, ed. and introduced by Ralph Manheim and John Willett. New York: Pantheon (Random House), 1969ff. [Also in Vintage paperback (1972ff). By far the best translation and edition in English.]
———. *Baal. Drei Fassungen*, ed. Dieter Schmidt. Frankfurt/M: Suhrkamp, 1966.
Die Bibel oder die ganze Heilige Schrift Neuen und Alten Testaments nach der deutschen Übersetzung Dr. Martin Luthers. St. Louis: Concordia, n.d.
———. Modernized edition: Boston: Massachusetts Bible Society—National Verlag Kompanie, 1967.

II. SECONDARY SOURCES

Bithell, Jethro. *Modern German Literature: 1880–1950*. London: Methuen, 1959.
Bloch, Ernst. *Entfremdung, Verfremdung*: Alienation, Estrangement." *Brecht*, ed. Erika Munk. New York: Bantam, 1972.
Brandt, Thomas O. "Brecht und die Bibel." *PMLA*, 79 (1964), 171–76.
———. *Die Vieldeutigkeit Bertolt Brechts*. Heidelberg: Lothar Stiehm, 1968.
Buchberger, Michael, ed. *Kirchliches Handlexikon*. Freiburg i. Br.: Herdersche Verlagshandlung, 1907.
Cabaniss, Allen. *Liturgy and Literature*. University, Alabama: University of Alabama Press, 1970.
Demetz, Peter, ed. *Brecht: A Collection of Critical Essays*. Englewood Cliffs, N.J.: Prentice-Hall, 1962.
Dostoevskii, Fedor Mikhailovich. *The Brothers Karamazov*, trans. Constance Garnett. New York: Modern Library, 1950.
Dumazeau, Henri. *Mère Courage [de] Brecht: Analyse critique*. Paris: Hatier, 1972.
Encyclopaedia Judaica. 16 vols. Jerusalem: Keter Publishing House/Macmillan, 1972.
Esslin, Martin. *Brecht: The Man and His Work*. New York: Doubleday, 1960. [Also Anchor Books paperback].
Ewen, Frederic. *Bertolt Brecht: His Life, His Art, and His Times*. New York: Citadel, 1967.

Frisch, Werner and Obermeier, K. W. *Brecht in Augsburg: Erinnerungen, Texte, Fotos; eine Dokumentation.* Frankfurt/M: Suhrkamp, 1976.

Garner, Gary Neil. "Bertolt Brecht's Use of the Bible and Christianity in Representative Dramatic Works." Diss., Louisiana State University, 1969.

Gilson, Etienne. *The Christian Philosophy of St. Thomas Aquinas.* New York: Random House, 1956.

_____. *God and Philosophy.* New Haven: Yale, 1941.

Ginsberg, Ernst. *Abschied, Erinnerungen, Theateraufsätze, Gedichte.* Zurich: Arche, 1965.

Goethe, Johann Wolfgang von. *Faust,* ed. Erich Trunz. Hamburg: Wegner, 1965.

Gray, Ronald. *Bertolt Brecht.* New York: Grove, 1961.

Grenzmann, Wilhelm. *Dichtung und Glaube: Probleme und Gestalten der deutschen Gegenwartsliteratur.* Frankfurt/M: Athenäum, 1967. [Though the author has an admirably encompassing point of view and definition of *Glaube,* and covers the spectrum from Benn to Andres, he fails to see any reason to include Brecht.]

Grimm, Reinhold. "Bertolt Brecht," in *Deutsche Dichter der Moderne,* ed. Benno von Wiese. Berlin: Erich Schmidt, 1965, pp. 528–54.

_____. *Bertolt Brecht.* Stuttgart: Metzlersche Verlagsbuchhandlung, 3rd ed., 1971.

_____. *Bertolt Brecht: Die Struktur seines Werkes.* Nürnberg: Hans Carl, 1962.

_____. *Bertolt Brecht und die Weltliteratur.* Nürnberg: Hans Carl, 1961.

_____. "Brecht's Beginnings." *The Drama Review,* 12 (Fall 1967), 22–35. Also in Munk, *Brecht.*

Hahn, Friedrich. *Bibel und moderne Literatur.* 4th ed. Stuttgart: Quell, 1969.

Hatfield, Henry. *Modern German Literature, The Major Figures in Context.* London: Edward Arnold, 1966.

Heller, Erich. *The Disinherited Mind: Essays in Modern German Literature and Thought.* New York: Farrar, Straus and Cudahy, 1957.

Heller, Peter. "Nihilist into Activist: Two Phases in the Development of Bertolt Brecht." *The Germanic Review,* 28 (1953), 144–55.

Högel, Max. *Bertolt Brecht: Ein Portrait.* Augsburg: Verlag der Schwäbischen Forschungsgemeinschaften, 1962.

Interpreter's Bible, The, ed. George Arthur Buttrick, et al. 12 vols. Nashville: Abingdon Press, 1956.

Jerome Biblical Commentary, The, ed. Raymond Brown, S.S., Joseph Fitzmeyer, S. J. and Roland Murphy, O. Carm. Englewood Cliffs, N.J.: Prentice-Hall, 1968.

Johst, Hanns. *Der Einsame: Ein Menschenuntergang.* Munich: Albert Langen, 1925. (First edition, Munich: Delphin, 1917).

Kesting, Marianne. *Bertolt Brecht in Selbstzeugnissen und Bilddokumenten.* Hamburg: Rowohlt, 1959.

Knust, Herbert. "Brecht's Dialektik vom Fressen und von der Moral." *Brecht Heute-Brecht Today,* 3 (1973), 221–50.

Kurz, S. J., Paul Konrad. *Über moderne Literatur.* Frankfurt/M: Joseph Knecht,

1969. Trans. Sr. Mary Frances McCarthy as *On Modern German Literature.* University, Alabama: University of Alabama Press, 1971.

Lewis, Beth Irwin. *George Grosz: Art and Politics in the Weimar Republic.* Madison: The University of Wisconsin Press, 1971. [This book contains some excellent Brecht-Grosz illustrative material, including the famous "Christ with the Gas Mask."]

Ley, Ralph J. "Brecht's Science and Cosmic Futility." *The Germanic Review,* 40 (1965), 205–24.

————. "The Marxist Ethos of Bertolt Brecht and its Relation to Existentialism: A Study of the Writer in the Scientific Age." Diss., Rutgers University, 1963.

Lubac, Henri de. *The Drama of Atheist Humanism,* trans. Edith M. Riley. New York: Sheed and Ward, 1950.

Maritain, Jacques. *Existence and the Existent,* trans. Lewis Galantiere and Gerald B. Phelan. New York: Pantheon, 1948.

————. *God and the Permission of Evil.* Milwaukee: Bruce, 1966.

Mayer, Hans. *Bertolt Brecht und die Tradition.* Pfullingen: Neske, 1961.

McKenzie, John L., S. J. *Dictionary of the Bible.* Milwaukee: Bruce, 1965.

Mews, Siegfried. "Bertolt Brecht and World Literature." *Papers on Language and Literature,* 13 (1977), 89–110.

————. "Biblical Themes and Motifs in Brecht's *Herr Puntila und sein Knecht Matti." The University of Dayton Review,* 13 (Spring 1979), 53–63.

Meyer-Lenz, D. P. "Brecht und der Pflaumenbaum." *Neu Deutsche Hefte,* 18, No. 1 (1971), pp. 40–48.

Michelsen, Peter. "Bertolt Brechts Atheismus." *Eckart,* 26 (1957), 48–56.

Milgram, Stanley. *Obedience to Authority: An Experimental View.* New York: Harper and Row, 1974.

Münsterer, Hans Otto. *Bert Brecht: Erinnerungen aus den Jahren 1917–1922.* Zurich: Arche, 1963.

Munk, Erika, ed. *Brecht.* New York: Bantam, 1972.

Murphy, G. Ronald. "Brecht's Pocket Bible." *The German Quarterly,* 50 (1977), 474–84.

Muschg, Walter. *Von Trakl zu Brecht: Dichter des Expressionismus.* Munich: Piper, 1961.

Nelson's Complete Concordance of the Revised Standard Version Bible, compiled under John W. Ellison. New York: Thomas Nelson, 1957.

Pabst, Hans. *Brecht und die Religion.* Graz: Styria, 1977.

Pinthus, Kurt, ed. *Menschheitsdämmerung: Ein Dokument des Expressionimus.* Hamburg: Rowohlt, 1959.

Rey, William H. "Theological Aesthetics?" *The Germanic Review,* 35 (1960), 243–61.

Rimbaud, Arthur. *A Season in Hell,* trans. and introduced by Delmore Schwartz. Norfolk, Conn.: New Directions, 1939.

Schmidt, Dieter. *Baal und der junge Brecht. Eine textkritische Untersuchung zur Entwicklung des Frühwerks.* Stuttgart: Metzler, 1966.

Sehm, Gunter G. "Moses, Christus und Paul Ackermann: Brechts *Aufstieg und Fall der Stadt Mahagonny."* *Brecht-Jahrbuch 1976* (Frankfurt/M: Suhrkamp, 1976), pp. 83–100.

Sokel, Walter H. *The Writer in Extremis: Expressionism in Twentieth Century Literature.* Stanford: Stanford University Press, 1959.

———. "Brecht's Split Characters and His Sense of the Tragic." *Brecht: A Collection of Critical Essays,* ed. Peter Demetz. Englewood Cliffs, N.J.: Prentice-Hall, 1962.

Völker, Klaus. *Brecht: A Biography,* trans. John Nowell. New York: Seabury Press, 1978.

Wilder, Amos N. *Theology and Modern Literature.* Cambridge: Harvard University Press, 1958. [This work is something of a classic, but unfortunately German literature is not extensively treated.]

Willett, John. *The Theatre of Bertolt Brecht: A Study from Eight Aspects.* 3rd rev. ed. New York: New Directions, 1968.

Woods, Barbara Allen. "The Function of Proverbs in Brecht." *Monatshefte,* 61 (1969), 49–57.

Wortkonkordanz: Sonderdruck aus dem Biblischen Nachschlagewerk zur Jubiläumsbibel. Stuttgart: Württembergische Bibelanstalt, 1963.

Ziolkowski, Theodore. *Fictional Transfigurations of Jesus.* Princeton: Princeton University Press, 1970. [Though Brecht is not directly considered, this work offers valuable parallels and good definitions.]

UNIVERSITY OF NORTH CAROLINA
STUDIES IN THE GERMANIC LANGUAGES
AND LITERATURES

For other volumes in the "Studies" see page ii and following page.

Send orders to: (U.S. and Canada)
The University of North Carolina Press, P. O. Box 2288
Chapel Hill, N.C. 27514
(All other countries) Feffer and Simons, Inc., 31 Union Square, New York, N.Y. 10003

UNIVERSITY OF NORTH CAROLINA
STUDIES IN THE GERMANIC LANGUAGES
AND LITERATURES

67 SIEGFRIED MEWS, ED. *Studies in German Literature of the Nineteenth and Twentieth Centuries. Festschrift for Frederic E. Coenen.* Foreword by Werner P. Friederich. 1970. 2nd ed. 1972. Pp. xx, 251.

68 JOHN NEUBAUER. *Bifocal Vision. Novalis' Philosophy of Nature and Disease.* 1971. Pp. x, 196.

69 VICTOR ANTHONY RUDOWSKI. *Lessing's* Aesthetica in Nuce. *An Analysis of the May 26, 1769, Letter to Nicolai.* 1971. Pp. xii, 146.

70 DONALD F. NELSON. *Portrait of the Artist as Hermes. A Study of Myth and Psychology in Thomas Mann's* Felix Krull. 1971. Pp. xii, 146.

71 MURRAY A. AND MARIAN L. COWIE, EDS. *The Works of Peter Schott (1460–1490).* Volume II: *Commentary.* Pp. xxix, 534. (See also volume 41.)

72 CHRISTINE OERTEL SJÖGREN. *The Marble Statue as Idea: Collected Essays on Adalbert Stifter's* Der Nachsommer. 1972. Pp. xiv, 121.

73 DONALD G. DAVIAU AND JORUN B. JOHNS, EDS. *The Correspondence of Arthur Schnitzler and Raoul Auernheimer with Raoul Auernheimer's Aphorisms.* 1972. Pp. xii, 161.

74 A. MARGARET ARENT MADELUNG. *The Laxdoela Saga: Its Structural Patterns.* 1972. Pp. xiv, 261.

75 JEFFREY L. SAMMONS. *Six Essays on the Young German Novel.* 2nd ed. 1975. Pp. xiv, 187.

76 DONALD H. CROSBY AND GEORGE C. SCHOOLFIELD, EDS. *Studies in the German Drama. A Festschrift in Honor of Walter Silz.* 1974. Pp. xxvi, 255.

77 J. W. THOMAS. *Tannhäuser: Poet and Legend. With Texts and Translation of his Works.* 1974. Pp. x, 202.

78 OLGA MARX AND ERNST MORWITZ, TRANS. *The Works of Stefan George.* 1974. 2nd, rev. and enl. ed. Pp. xxviii, 431.

79 SIEGFRIED MEWS AND HERBERT KNUST, EDS. *Essays on Brecht: Theater and Politics.* 1974. Pp. xiv, 241.

80 DONALD G. DAVIAU AND GEORGE J. BUELOW. *The* Ariadne auf Naxos *of Hugo von Hofmannsthal and Richard Strauss.* 1975. Pp. x, 274.

81 ELAINE E. BONEY. *Rainer Maria Rilke:* Duinesian Elegies. *German Text with English Translation and Commentary.* 2nd ed. 1977. Pp. xii, 153.

For other volumes in the "Studies" see preceding page and p. ii.

Send orders to: (U.S. and Canada)
The University of North Carolina Press, P. O. Box 2288
Chapel Hill, N.C. 27514
(All other countries) Feffer and Simons, Inc., 31 Union Square, New York, N.Y. 10003

Volumes 1–44 and 46–49 of the "Studies" have been reprinted.
They may be ordered from:
AMS Press, Inc., 56 E. 13th Street, New York, N.Y. 10003
For a complete list of reprinted titles write to:
Editor, UNCSGL&L, 442 Dey Hall, 014A, UNC, Chapel Hill, N.C. 27514